Law of Attraction

GRATITUDE JOURNAL

*Attract More of What **YOU** Want to Create a Happy Abundant Life!*

Dana Smithers

Law of Attraction Gratitude Journal
Copyright © 2017 Dana Smithers
All rights reserved.

No part of this publication may be reproduced or transmitted in any form or by any means, electronic or mechanical including photocopying, recording or any other information storage retrieval system without permission from the author.

While the Law of Attraction and other techniques discussed in this book are simple to use and have produced remarkable results, they must be used at your own risk. The author cannot guarantee any specific results and reminds the reader to take responsibility for their use of these techniques.

Dana J. Smithers can be reached at:
Info@DanaSmithers.com
Website: www.DanaSmithers.com

Printed in the United States.

ISBN – 978-1542927376

ACKNOWELDGEMENTS

I would like to thank my husband for always supporting me in what makes me truly happy.

I would also like to express my complete gratitude to Michael J. Losier for attracting me and for me attracting him into my life. Michael is 'The Boss' when it comes to living a rich, delicious, juicy life through deliberate attracting.

TABLE OF CONTENTS

What the Law of Attraction Is & How to Deliberately Use It 1
Why Expressing Gratitude is Key to Your Happiness 2
The ASK~BELIEVE~RECEIVE Process 3
How to Benefit the Most from Your Gratitude Journal. 4
WEEK 1: Reset Your Vibration By Asking "So, What Do I Want?" 6
WEEK 2: When Negative Emotions Come Up, Deal With Them Briefly 10
WEEK 3: Set Your Intention For The Day, Then Segment Intentions 14
WEEK 4: Time To Let Your Low-Vibe Friends Go 18
WEEK 5: Positive Thoughts Can Turn Into Negative Attraction 22
WEEK 6: The Law of Attraction's Job Is To Match Vibrations 26
WEEK 7: Identify Your Desire By Deciding What You Don't Want 30
WEEK 8: Identify Your Desire And Focus On What You Do Want 34
WEEK 9: Create A Visual Of What You Want To Manifest 38
WEEK 10: Stop Attracting Negative People By Changing Your Vibration 42
WEEK 11: Take Ownership Of Everything You Attract 46
WEEK 12: Three Words To Avoid 'Don't Not No' 50
WEEK 13: Whining Only Gets You More Of What You Don't Want 54
WEEK 14: Take Action When It Feels Right To You 58
WEEK 15: Consider Yourself Employable 62
WEEK 16: Change Your Affirmations To "I Am In The Process Of" 66
WEEK 17: Give Your Attention To What You Want To Change 70
WEEK 18: Wishing To Win The Lottery May Never Happen For You 74
WEEK 19: Negative Self-Talk Stops When You Stop Believing It 78
WEEK 20: Abundance Is A Feeling And Not A Thing 82
WEEK 21: Raise Your Vibration By Staying Focused On What You Want 86
WEEK 22: Your Vibrational Bubble Contains All Your Thoughts 90
WEEK 23: Other People Can Drain Your Energy If You Are Not Mindful 94
WEEK 24: Look For Evidence That What You Want Is Possible 98

WEEK 25: You Are Only Responsible For Your Own Vibration 102

WEEK 26: Have an Attitude of Gratitude 106

WEEK 27: Saying 'No' Without Using The Word 'No' 110

WEEK 28: You Can Change Existing Relationships 114

WEEK 29: Using The Statement "I've Decided" Is Powerful 118

WEEK 30: It's Better To Release Weight Than To Lose It 122

WEEK 31: Being Selfish Is Just Good Self-Care 126

WEEK 32: Change Your Words So Your Vibes Change 130

WEEK 33: Become More Positive By Being Less Negative 134

WEEK 34: The Law of Attraction Brings You What You Need 138

WEEK 35: Want A Different Result? Get A Different Vibe! 142

WEEK 36: Vision Boards Work When You Believe They Do 146

WEEK 37: A Vibrational Business Plan Works 150

WEEK 38: Create Desire Statements That Resonate With You 154

WEEK 39: The Manifesting Equation 158

WEEK 40: Being Mindful Attracts More of What You Want 162

WEEK 41: Look At All Your Law of Attraction Receipts 166

WEEK 42: Celebrate The Closeness Of The Match 170

WEEK 43: When Resistance Comes Up In Relationships 174

WEEK 44: The More Resistance You Have The More It Persists 178

WEEK 45: Whatever You Believe You Can Achieve – You Will 182

WEEK 46: Focus On How You Will Feel When You Have What You Desire . 186

WEEK 47: Find A Positive Focus In A Negative Situation 190

WEEK 48: Let Go Of Beliefs That No Longer Serve You 194

WEEK 49: Model The Behaviour You Would Like To See In Others 198

WEEK 50: Ask For What You Want And Be Open 202

WEEK 51: Positive Thoughts Attract More Positive Thoughts 206

WEEK 52: Celebrate Your Success 210

What I Discovered About Myself, Gratitude & The Law Of Attraction 214

About the Author 216

WHAT THE LAW OF ATTRACTION IS HOW TO DELIBERATELY USE IT

What the Law of Attraction Is...

The **'Law of Attraction'** is based on the science of quantum physics. It is an unseen powerful energetic force that attracts similar vibrations. Everything is energy including your thoughts, and your thoughts are what starts the attracting or manifesting process.

A simple way to grasp this is to consider the 'Words = Results Relationship'. Everything that you want to manifest starts with your words, from here your words form thoughts, and those thoughts give off a 'vibe' or a vibration that is either positive or negative. The result or manifestation you then receive is based on this relationship.

The "WORDS = RESULTS" Relationship

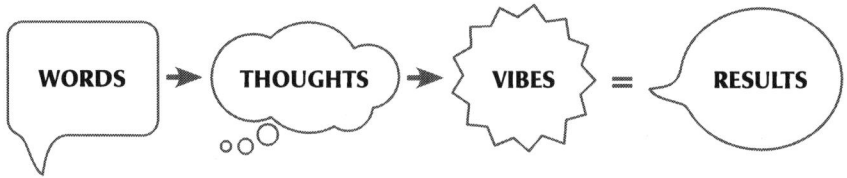

How to Deliberately Use the Law of Attraction...

To be what is called a **'Deliberate Attractor'** is to consciously be aware of your words, thoughts, the positive or negative vibes that come from your thoughts, and then observe the result you achieve. If you do not like your result then you need to go back to the beginning and change your words, which will change your thoughts, which will change your mood or feeling and eventually change your result!

WHY EXPRESSING GRATITUDE IS *Key* TO YOUR HAPPINESS

When things are going well in your life you most likely feel happy or in law of attraction lingo – you're giving off positive vibes. And those positive vibes you are giving off just keep on attracting more positive thoughts, feelings, people and/or circumstances in your life. You probably feel grateful about what you are attracting and even take credit for all the positivity surrounding you.

Your feeling grateful is what attracts more happiness into your life.

And conversely, when things aren't going so well you may notice that you feel badly. You may even complain and you might even notice that a day that started off badly only got worse and you wished that day was over!

One expression of Gratitude raises your vibration. That vibration increases your ability to attract more. Like vibrations attract more like vibrations.

If you do find yourself in a negative mindset, you can shift that into a positive mindset by asking yourself "So, what do I want?" and then focus on that … only.

THE
Ask ~ Believe ~ Receive
PROCESS

1. **ASK** ~ the Law of Attraction will respond to what you **ASK** for by you having **CLARITY** about what you want. Be as specific as you can. Focus on 1 ASK until you have manifested that. It often works better if you create a list of what you 'Don't Want' and then your list of what you 'Do Want.' Once you have gone through the process and manifested that **ASK**, then move on to your next **ASK**.

2. **BELIEVE** ~ you must **BELIEVE** that what you want to manifest is possible. Start looking for the **EVIDENCE** around you that confirms what you want to have – is possible. Remove as much doubt as you can by getting rid of negative vibrations. How you **FEEL** about what you say you believe is as important as your belief around your belief!

3. **RECEIVE** ~ the Law of Attraction will start giving you what you need to do, know or have to manifest your **ASK**. Your part is to celebrate the **CLOSENESS** of the **MATCH**. You need to be able to **RECEIVE** whatever you attract. Your positive vibration around what you attracted regardless of how small or non-perfect what you attracted is – express gratitude and then say "Next"! Start observing what you do receive and how you react to it.

HOW TO BENEFIT THE MOST *from* YOUR GRATITUDE JOURNAL

You most likely live a pretty busy life. This 52 week Gratitude Journal has been created so that you only need about 30 – 60 minutes a week to journal. Find a quiet space and give yourself this gift of time with all the attention on you.

The intention is to make expressing Gratitude a daily habit, and for you to start using the Law of Attraction deliberately - daily.

The Gratitude Journal is set up to allow your thoughts to flow easily from one page to the next.

- Starting with a **Law of Attraction TIP** that sets the 'Weekly Theme'

- Then, **5 Statements** where you will set your **'Intention'**, express what you are **'Most Grateful For'**, notice where you **'Deliberately'** used the Law of Attraction in your week, use the Law of Attraction style affirmation of **"I am in the process of…"** and write about how you **'Feel'** when you give off positive vibes

- The **'Ask~Believe~Receive'** process where you will need to get clarity on what you want – your ASK; look for evidence and remove doubt about what you BELIEVE is possible; and pay attention to what you manifest and RECEIVE

- Finally making a list of where you see **Abundance** showing up in your life

Date: ____ /____ /20____

WEEK 1

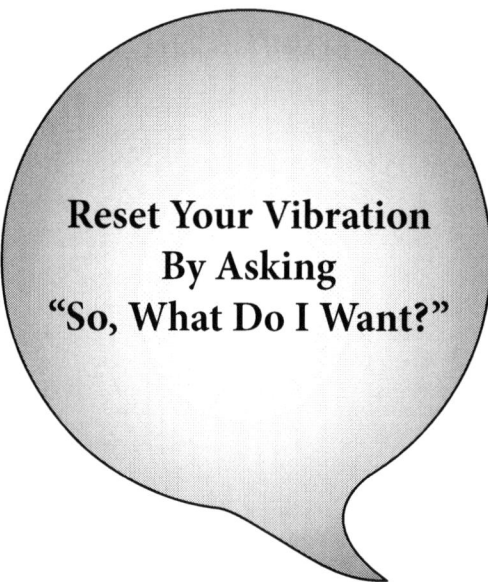

Reset Your Vibration By Asking "So, What Do I Want?"

When you have a negative vibration the quickest and easiest way to 'reset' your vibration is by asking yourself or someone else who has a negative vibration *"So what do I (you) want?"*

The focus is now on the positive thought about what you want and will attract a positive vibration.

That one positive thought can shift your energy enough so that you keep on attracting more positive situations. The law of attraction is interested in giving you what you need to do, know or have.

1. My **INTENTION** for this week (around relationships, money, health, career and/or business) is …

_____
_____
_____
_____

2. Last week I felt **MOST GRATEFUL** for …

_____
_____
_____
_____

3. I **DELIBERATELY** used the Law of Attraction to attract…

_____
_____
_____
_____

4. I am **IN THE PROCESS** of manifesting…

_____
_____
_____
_____

5. I **FELT** major **POSITIVE VIBES** last week when …

_____
_____
_____
_____

THE
Ask ~ Believe ~ Receive
PROCESS

1. My **ASK** for this week is…

___
___
___
___

2. The **EVIDENCE** to support what I **BELIEVE** is possible looks like this…

___
___
___
___

3. I was excited to **RECEIVE** (fill in the blank) last week…

___
___
___
___

ABUNDANCE IS A FEELING

Make a list of all the ways you felt or observed
ABUNDANCE in your life last week…

_____   _____
_____   _____
_____   _____
_____   _____
_____   _____
_____   _____
_____   _____
_____   _____
_____   _____
_____   _____
_____   _____
_____   _____
_____   _____
_____   _____
_____   _____

Date: ____ /____ /20____

WEEK 2

When Negative Emotions Come Up, Deal With Them Briefly

We all have negative emotions. Some people seem to attract more than others and there is a reason for that.

The more you focus on how mad, sad or badly you feel, the more of the same will come to you. And, the more you tell others the more you attract!

So have your hissy fit and do whatever it takes for you to get that negative energy out of your body…but *do it briefly*.

Only you can decide how brief 'briefly' is for you.

1. My **INTENTION** for this week (around relationships, money, health, career and/or business) is …

_____
_____
_____
_____

2. Last week I felt **MOST GRATEFUL** for …

_____
_____
_____
_____

3. I **DELIBERATELY** used the Law of Attraction to attract…

_____
_____
_____
_____

4. I am **IN THE PROCESS** of manifesting…

_____
_____
_____
_____

5. I **FELT** major **POSITIVE VIBES** last week when …

_____
_____
_____
_____

THE
Ask ~ Believe ~ Receive
PROCESS

1. My **ASK** for this week is…

_____
_____
_____
_____

2. The **EVIDENCE** to support what I **BELIEVE** is possible looks like this…

_____
_____
_____
_____

3. I was excited to **RECEIVE** (fill in the blank) last week…

_____
_____
_____
_____

ABUNDANCE IS A FEELING

Make a list of all the ways you felt or observed
ABUNDANCE in your life last week…

_____   _____
_____   _____
_____   _____
_____   _____
_____   _____
_____   _____
_____   _____
_____   _____
_____   _____
_____   _____
_____   _____
_____   _____
_____   _____
_____   _____

Date: ____ / ____ /20____

WEEK 3

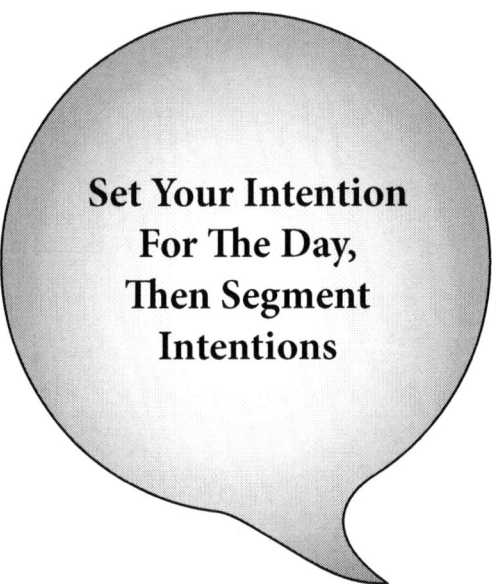

Set Your Intention For The Day, Then Segment Intentions

One of the best ways to have a great day is to start by setting your 'Intention'. What do you want the day to look like? Who do you want to meet? What can you do today that will make you happy?

Be specific. The law of attraction likes details.

Remember to set your intention again throughout the day, in segments, as your day starts to unfold. You may find you want to stick with your original intention or you might decide to change it.

1. My **INTENTION** for this week (around relationships, money, health, career and/or business) is ...

_____
_____
_____
_____

2. Last week I felt **MOST GRATEFUL** for ...

_____
_____
_____
_____

3. I **DELIBERATELY** used the Law of Attraction to attract...

_____
_____
_____
_____

4. I am **IN THE PROCESS** of manifesting...

_____
_____
_____
_____

5. I **FELT** major **POSITIVE VIBES** last week when ...

_____
_____
_____
_____

THE
Ask ~ Believe ~ Receive
PROCESS

1. My **ASK** for this week is…

_____
_____
_____
_____

2. The **EVIDENCE** to support what I **BELIEVE** is possible looks like this…

_____
_____
_____
_____

3. I was excited to **RECEIVE** (fill in the blank) last week…

_____
_____
_____
_____

ABUNDANCE IS A FEELING

Make a list of all the ways you felt or observed
ABUNDANCE in your life last week…

_____   _____
_____   _____
_____   _____
_____   _____
_____   _____
_____   _____
_____   _____
_____   _____
_____   _____
_____   _____
_____   _____
_____   _____
_____   _____
_____   _____

Date: ____ /____ /20____

WEEK 4

Time To Let Your Low-Vibe Friends Go

People come into your life for 'a reason, a season or a lifetime'.

And you may find that you want to let some of those people go who seem to constantly drag you down - aka negative energy vampire drainers.

The best way to let these low-vibe friends go is by *lovingly wish them well* on their journey.

Find something good to remember them by and then focus on the kind of high-vibe people you want to attract into your life now.

1. My **INTENTION** for this week (around relationships, money, health, career and/or business) is …

_____
_____
_____
_____

2. Last week I felt **MOST GRATEFUL** for …

_____
_____
_____
_____

3. I **DELIBERATELY** used the Law of Attraction to attract…

_____
_____
_____
_____

4. I am **IN THE PROCESS** of manifesting…

_____
_____
_____
_____

5. I **FELT** major **POSITIVE VIBES** last week when …

_____
_____
_____
_____

THE
Ask ~ Believe ~ Receive
PROCESS

1. My **ASK** for this week is…

   _____
   _____
   _____
   _____

2. The **EVIDENCE** to support what I **BELIEVE** is possible looks like this…

   _____
   _____
   _____
   _____

3. I was excited to **RECEIVE** (fill in the blank) last week…

   _____
   _____
   _____
   _____

ABUNDANCE IS A FEELING

Make a list of all the ways you felt or observed
ABUNDANCE in your life last week…

_____   _____
_____   _____
_____   _____
_____   _____
_____   _____
_____   _____
_____   _____
_____   _____
_____   _____
_____   _____
_____   _____
_____   _____
_____   _____
_____   _____

Date: ____ / ____ /20____

WEEK 5

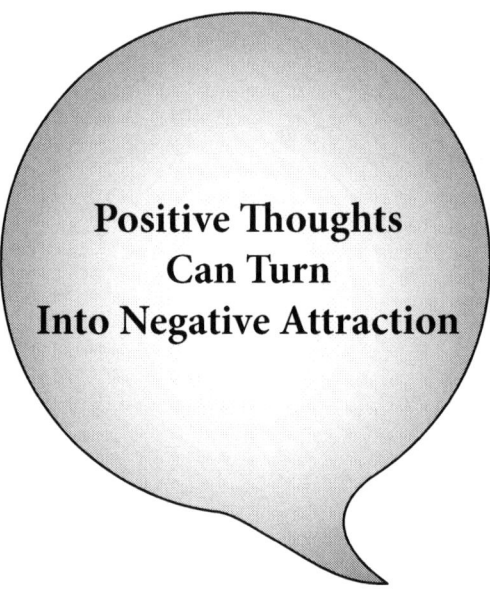

Positive Thoughts Can Turn Into Negative Attraction

This may seem hard to grasp but if you have a positive thought and you get frustrated because you haven't attracted or manifested what you wanted, you are now sending out negative vibrations.

Negative vibrations attract more negative vibrations

So the best thing to do for you to do is to go back to your positive thought. Visualize what you want to manifest so you feel good about it.

Give it more time by 'allowing' the law of attraction to get everything in order for your manifesting.

1. My **INTENTION** for this week (around relationships, money, health, career and/or business) is …

_____
_____
_____
_____

2. Last week I felt **MOST GRATEFUL** for …

_____
_____
_____
_____

3. I **DELIBERATELY** used the Law of Attraction to attract…

_____
_____
_____
_____

4. I am **IN THE PROCESS** of manifesting…

_____
_____
_____
_____

5. I **FELT** major **POSITIVE VIBES** last week when …

_____
_____
_____
_____

THE
Ask ~ Believe ~ Receive
PROCESS

1. My **ASK** for this week is…

_____

_____

_____

_____

2. The **EVIDENCE** to support what I **BELIEVE** is possible looks like this…

_____

_____

_____

_____

3. I was excited to **RECEIVE** (fill in the blank) last week…

_____

_____

_____

_____

ABUNDANCE IS A FEELING

Make a list of all the ways you felt or observed
ABUNDANCE in your life last week…

_____   _____
_____   _____
_____   _____
_____   _____
_____   _____
_____   _____
_____   _____
_____   _____
_____   _____
_____   _____
_____   _____
_____   _____
_____   _____
_____   _____
_____   _____

Date: ____ / ____ /20____

WEEK 6

The Law of Attraction's Job Is To Match Vibrations

By now you have probably started to notice what you are attracting on a daily basis. And you probably like some of what you are attracting and dislike some of what you are attracting.

The law of attraction is obedient and has a simple job description which is to…

> Match Vibrations

This is why it is so important for you to remember the 'Words=Results Relationship'.

Every word you say, thought you have, feeling or vibration from that thought is matched by the law of attraction.

1. My **INTENTION** for this week (around relationships, money, health, career and/or business) is …

_____
_____
_____
_____

2. Last week I felt **MOST GRATEFUL** for …

_____
_____
_____
_____

3. I **DELIBERATELY** used the Law of Attraction to attract…

_____
_____
_____
_____

4. I am **IN THE PROCESS** of manifesting…

_____
_____
_____
_____

5. I **FELT** major **POSITIVE VIBES** last week when …

_____
_____
_____
_____

THE
Ask ~ Believe ~ Receive
PROCESS

1. My **ASK** for this week is…

_____
_____
_____
_____

2. The **EVIDENCE** to support what I **BELIEVE** is possible looks like this…

_____
_____
_____
_____

3. I was excited to **RECEIVE** (fill in the blank) last week…

_____
_____
_____
_____

ABUNDANCE IS A FEELING

Make a list of all the ways you felt or observed
ABUNDANCE in your life last week…

Date: ____ / ____ /20____

WEEK 7

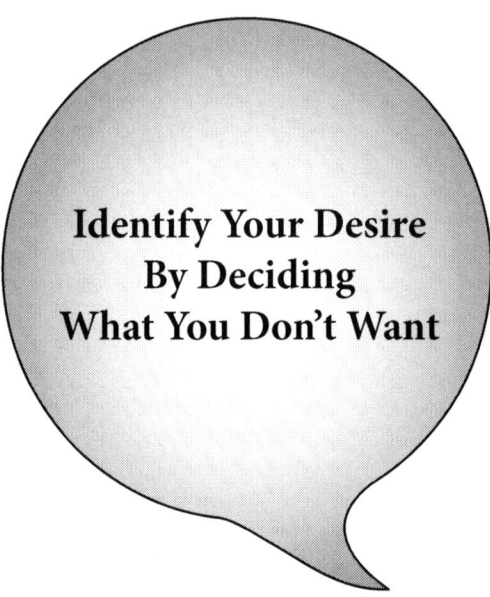

Identify Your Desire By Deciding What You Don't Want

You may not realize it but you are constantly deciding on what you do want by knowing what you don't want.

This is called getting *'Clarity' from 'Contrast'*. When you are looking for a partner you decide what you do want by knowing what you don't want.

When you are out shopping for something you are constantly saying 'no' to what you don't want, and 'yes' to what you do want.

Make a list called 'Don't Want' and another list 'Do Want'; focus only on the 'Do Want' list.

1. My **INTENTION** for this week (around relationships, money, health, career and/or business) is …

_____
_____
_____
_____

2. Last week I felt **MOST GRATEFUL** for …

_____
_____
_____
_____

3. I **DELIBERATELY** used the Law of Attraction to attract…

_____
_____
_____
_____

4. I am **IN THE PROCESS** of manifesting…

_____
_____
_____
_____

5. I **FELT** major **POSITIVE VIBES** last week when …

_____
_____
_____
_____

THE
Ask ~ Believe ~ Receive
PROCESS

1. My **ASK** for this week is…

_____
_____
_____
_____

2. The **EVIDENCE** to support what I **BELIEVE** is possible looks like this…

_____
_____
_____
_____

3. I was excited to **RECEIVE** (fill in the blank) last week…

_____
_____
_____
_____

ABUNDANCE IS A FEELING

Make a list of all the ways you felt or observed
ABUNDANCE in your life last week…

_____   _____
_____   _____
_____   _____
_____   _____
_____   _____
_____   _____
_____   _____
_____   _____
_____   _____
_____   _____
_____   _____
_____   _____
_____   _____
_____   _____
_____   _____
_____   _____

Date: ____ / ____ /20____

WEEK 8

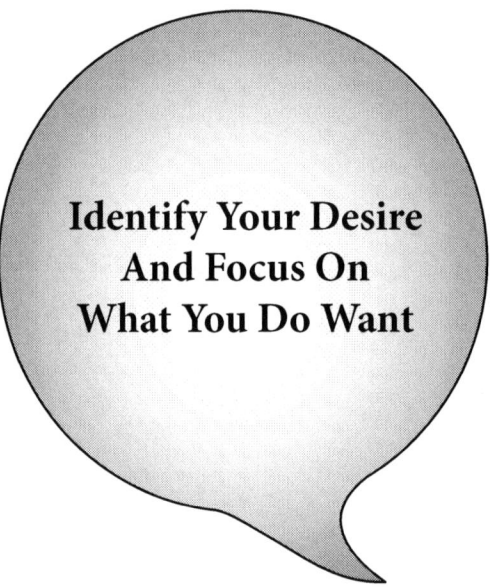

Identify Your Desire And Focus On What You Do Want

Once you've completed your 'Do Want' list you can now start focusing on attracting things, people or situations that are on your list.

Your entire focus now is on what you want so you have your non-negotiable list for anything that comes your way.

Now when you attract something that you don't want, you only have to briefly expend a small amount of energy to say 'no' to it.

The rest of your energy is freed up to *focus on what you do want* to attract.

1. My **INTENTION** for this week (around relationships, money, health, career and/or business) is …

_____
_____
_____
_____

2. Last week I felt **MOST GRATEFUL** for …

_____
_____
_____
_____

3. I **DELIBERATELY** used the Law of Attraction to attract…

_____
_____
_____
_____

4. I am **IN THE PROCESS** of manifesting…

_____
_____
_____
_____

5. I **FELT** major **POSITIVE VIBES** last week when …

_____
_____
_____
_____

THE
Ask ~ Believe ~ Receive
PROCESS

1. My **ASK** for this week is…

_____
_____
_____
_____

2. The **EVIDENCE** to support what I **BELIEVE** is possible looks like this…

_____
_____
_____
_____

3. I was excited to **RECEIVE** (fill in the blank) last week…

_____
_____
_____
_____

ABUNDANCE IS A FEELING

Make a list of all the ways you felt or observed
ABUNDANCE in your life last week…

_____   _____
_____   _____
_____   _____
_____   _____
_____   _____
_____   _____
_____   _____
_____   _____
_____   _____
_____   _____
_____   _____
_____   _____
_____   _____
_____   _____

Date: ____ /____ /20____

WEEK 9

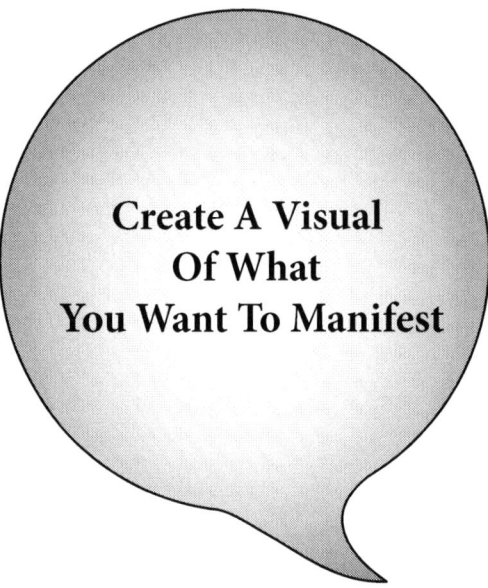

Create A Visual Of What You Want To Manifest

Did you know that by *creating a visual* of what you want, you can speed up the manifesting process?

You might be someone who likes to create a Vision Board or you might be someone who likes to write things down. It doesn't matter how you want to express what you desire but it does matter that you take time to 'visualize' what you want.

And it's equally important that you look at that on a daily basis so it is uppermost in your mind.

1. My **INTENTION** for this week (around relationships, money, health, career and/or business) is …

_____
_____
_____
_____

2. Last week I felt **MOST GRATEFUL** for …

_____
_____
_____
_____

3. I **DELIBERATELY** used the Law of Attraction to attract…

_____
_____
_____
_____

4. I am **IN THE PROCESS** of manifesting…

_____
_____
_____
_____

5. I **FELT** major **POSITIVE VIBES** last week when …

_____
_____
_____
_____

THE
Ask ~ Believe ~ Receive
PROCESS

1. My **ASK** for this week is…

2. The **EVIDENCE** to support what I **BELIEVE** is possible looks like this…

3. I was excited to **RECEIVE** (fill in the blank) last week…

ABUNDANCE IS A FEELING

Make a list of all the ways you felt or observed
ABUNDANCE in your life last week…

_____   _____
_____   _____
_____   _____
_____   _____
_____   _____
_____   _____
_____   _____
_____   _____
_____   _____
_____   _____
_____   _____
_____   _____
_____   _____
_____   _____

Date: ____ /____ /20____

WEEK 10

Stop Attracting Negative People By Changing Your Vibration

We all attract negative people sometime in our life. What's most important is that you recognize this so that you can consciously change your vibration.

> It's up to you to make having a positive vibration a habit

Whenever you come across a negative person ask yourself "So what do I want in this situation?"

You may have to let them go, or let them know you want to focus on the positive things in life. You can still 'briefly' talk about their challenges but keep it short.

1. My **INTENTION** for this week (around relationships, money, health, career and/or business) is …

_____
_____
_____
_____

2. Last week I felt **MOST GRATEFUL** for …

_____
_____
_____
_____

3. I **DELIBERATELY** used the Law of Attraction to attract…

_____
_____
_____
_____

4. I am **IN THE PROCESS** of manifesting…

_____
_____
_____
_____

5. I **FELT** major **POSITIVE VIBES** last week when …

_____
_____
_____
_____

THE
Ask ~ Believe ~ Receive
PROCESS

1. My **ASK** for this week is…

_____
_____
_____
_____

2. The **EVIDENCE** to support what I **BELIEVE** is possible looks like this…

_____
_____
_____
_____

3. I was excited to **RECEIVE** (fill in the blank) last week…

_____
_____
_____
_____

ABUNDANCE IS A FEELING

Make a list of all the ways you felt or observed
ABUNDANCE in your life last week…

Date: ____ / ____ /20____

WEEK 11

Take Ownership Of Everything You Attract

You might be someone who loves to take ownership of all the good you attract in your life. And then when the negative not-so-good stuff happens you might want to blame someone or something and even wonder where did that come from.

You are not a bad person
because you attract negative things

Just be mindful of what you are watching or listening to that sends negative messages to your subconscious.

And then make a conscious choice to look at what you can learn from the situation.

1. My **INTENTION** for this week (around relationships, money, health, career and/or business) is …

_____
_____
_____
_____

2. Last week I felt **MOST GRATEFUL** for …

_____
_____
_____
_____

3. I **DELIBERATELY** used the Law of Attraction to attract…

_____
_____
_____
_____

4. I am **IN THE PROCESS** of manifesting…

_____
_____
_____
_____

5. I **FELT** major **POSITIVE VIBES** last week when …

_____
_____
_____
_____

THE
Ask ~ Believe ~ Receive
PROCESS

1. My **ASK** for this week is…

   _____
   _____
   _____
   _____

2. The **EVIDENCE** to support what I **BELIEVE** is possible looks like this…

   _____
   _____
   _____
   _____

3. I was excited to **RECEIVE** (fill in the blank) last week…

   _____
   _____
   _____
   _____

ABUNDANCE IS A FEELING

Make a list of all the ways you felt or observed
ABUNDANCE in your life last week…

_____	_____
_____	_____
_____	_____
_____	_____
_____	_____
_____	_____
_____	_____
_____	_____
_____	_____
_____	_____
_____	_____
_____	_____
_____	_____
_____	_____
_____	_____
_____	_____

Date: ____ / ____ /20____

WEEK 12

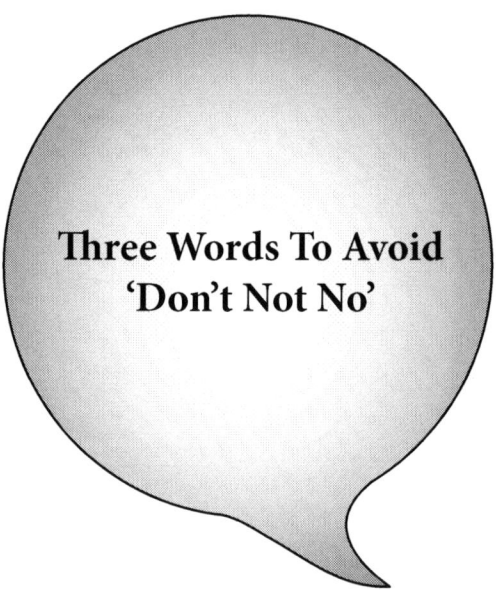

Now that you are understanding how the law of attraction works you know that you can deliberately attract more of what you want.

Another great tip for attracting more of what you want is to limit or avoid the use of…

      Don't   Not   No

The reason for this is because each of these words is 1) negative and 2) our subconscious deletes the 'don't not and no' and the focus is on the rest of the sentence.

Try this: Don't think of the Eiffel Tower of Paris.

1. My **INTENTION** for this week (around relationships, money, health, career and/or business) is …

_____
_____
_____
_____

2. Last week I felt **MOST GRATEFUL** for …

_____
_____
_____
_____

3. I **DELIBERATELY** used the Law of Attraction to attract…

_____
_____
_____
_____

4. I am **IN THE PROCESS** of manifesting…

_____
_____
_____
_____

5. I **FELT** major **POSITIVE VIBES** last week when …

_____
_____
_____
_____

THE
Ask ~ Believe ~ Receive
PROCESS

1. My **ASK** for this week is…

   _____
   _____
   _____
   _____

2. The **EVIDENCE** to support what I **BELIEVE** is possible looks like this…

   _____
   _____
   _____
   _____

3. I was excited to **RECEIVE** (fill in the blank) last week…

   _____
   _____
   _____
   _____

ABUNDANCE IS A FEELING

Make a list of all the ways you felt or observed
ABUNDANCE in your life last week…

_____   _____
_____   _____
_____   _____
_____   _____
_____   _____
_____   _____
_____   _____
_____   _____
_____   _____
_____   _____
_____   _____
_____   _____
_____   _____
_____   _____
_____   _____

Date: ____ /____ /20____

WEEK 13

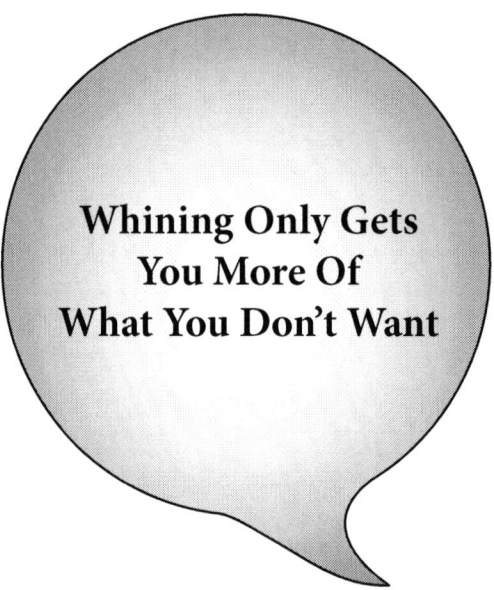

Whether you have young children who whine a lot, or know someone who whines a lot, or maybe you might be someone who whines a lot - regardless, all that whining is wearing!

All those negative emotions only attract more negative vibrations and on and on it goes.

This is where you need to remind yourself to ask the 'reset vibe' question of "So what do I (they) want?"

Change the focus to the flip side of the 'whining' situation. How can you get to a better positive outcome?

1. My **INTENTION** for this week (around relationships, money, health, career and/or business) is …

2. Last week I felt **MOST GRATEFUL** for …

3. I **DELIBERATELY** used the Law of Attraction to attract…

4. I am **IN THE PROCESS** of manifesting…

5. I **FELT** major **POSITIVE VIBES** last week when …

THE
Ask ~ Believe ~ Receive
PROCESS

1. My **ASK** for this week is…

_____
_____
_____
_____

2. The **EVIDENCE** to support what I **BELIEVE** is possible looks like this…

_____
_____
_____
_____

3. I was excited to **RECEIVE** (fill in the blank) last week…

_____
_____
_____
_____

ABUNDANCE IS A FEELING

Make a list of all the ways you felt or observed
ABUNDANCE in your life last week…

Date: ____ /____ /20____

WEEK 14

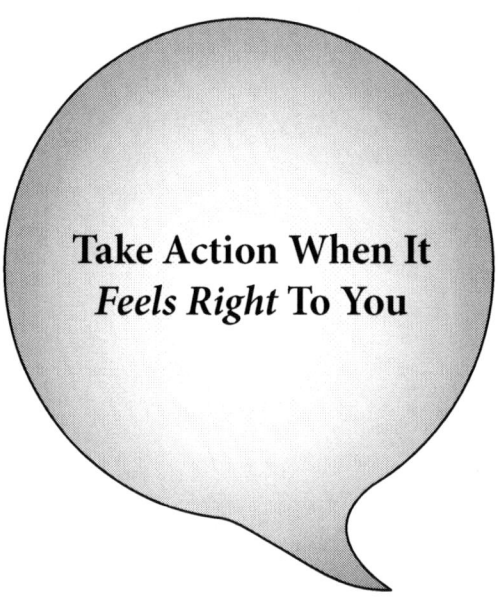

Take Action When It *Feels Right* To You

By now you are familiar with the 3 Step 'Ask Believe Receive' process. You know that you 1) Get Clarity On Your Desire 2) Look For Evidence and Remove Doubt and 3) Observe the Closeness of the Matches.

And while you are waiting for the law of attraction to bring you everything you need to do, know or have, only take action when it …

FEELS RIGHT

Wait for the law of attraction do its work or you may derail your desires in your enthusiasm. Be patient.

1. My **INTENTION** for this week (around relationships, money, health, career and/or business) is ...

_____
_____
_____
_____

2. Last week I felt **MOST GRATEFUL** for ...

_____
_____
_____
_____

3. I **DELIBERATELY** used the Law of Attraction to attract...

_____
_____
_____
_____

4. I am **IN THE PROCESS** of manifesting...

_____
_____
_____
_____

5. I **FELT** major **POSITIVE VIBES** last week when ...

_____
_____
_____
_____

THE
Ask ~ Believe ~ Receive
PROCESS

1. My **ASK** for this week is…

_____
_____
_____
_____

2. The **EVIDENCE** to support what I **BELIEVE** is possible looks like this…

_____
_____
_____
_____

3. I was excited to **RECEIVE** (fill in the blank) last week…

_____
_____
_____
_____

ABUNDANCE IS A FEELING

Make a list of all the ways you felt or observed
ABUNDANCE in your life last week…

_____	_____
_____	_____
_____	_____
_____	_____
_____	_____
_____	_____
_____	_____
_____	_____
_____	_____
_____	_____
_____	_____
_____	_____

Date: ____ /____ /20____

WEEK 15

Consider Yourself Employable

When you hear the word 'unemployed' it often contains a negative connotation or vibration to it. Your mind might focus on all the 'lack' that surrounds someone who is unemployed.

If this is you, or someone you know who is looking for work, it is very important that you, or they understand you or they are …

Employable

When you say someone is employable it immediately shifts the energy to a positive focus. The 'un' in the word unemployable is negative and therefore will attract more negative energy.

1. My **INTENTION** for this week (around relationships, money, health, career and/or business) is …

_____
_____
_____
_____

2. Last week I felt **MOST GRATEFUL** for …

_____
_____
_____
_____

3. I **DELIBERATELY** used the Law of Attraction to attract…

_____
_____
_____
_____

4. I am **IN THE PROCESS** of manifesting…

_____
_____
_____
_____

5. I **FELT** major **POSITIVE VIBES** last week when …

_____
_____
_____
_____

THE
Ask ~ Believe ~ Receive
PROCESS

1. My **ASK** for this week is…

_____
_____
_____
_____

2. The **EVIDENCE** to support what I **BELIEVE** is possible looks like this…

_____
_____
_____
_____

3. I was excited to **RECEIVE** (fill in the blank) last week…

_____
_____
_____
_____

ABUNDANCE IS A FEELING

Make a list of all the ways you felt or observed
ABUNDANCE in your life last week…

Date: ____ / ____ /20____

WEEK 16

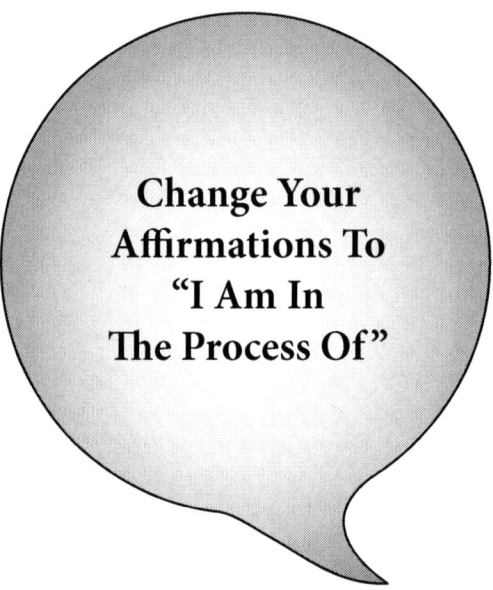

Change Your Affirmations To "I Am In The Process Of"

An affirmation is a declarative sentence written or spoken in the present tense. It is affirming that what you want to do or have, is going to happen for you.

But here's the kicker…you can say or think all the affirmations in the world but if you do not believe what you are saying is true or possible, it will never happen for you.

Try this from the law of attraction instead.

I am in the process of…
(complete with what you want to do or have)

1. My **INTENTION** for this week (around relationships, money, health, career and/or business) is ...

_____
_____
_____
_____

2. Last week I felt **MOST GRATEFUL** for ...

_____
_____
_____
_____

3. I **DELIBERATELY** used the Law of Attraction to attract...

_____
_____
_____
_____

4. I am **IN THE PROCESS** of manifesting...

_____
_____
_____
_____

5. I **FELT** major **POSITIVE VIBES** last week when ...

_____
_____
_____
_____

THE
Ask ~ Believe ~ Receive
PROCESS

1. My **ASK** for this week is…

_____
_____
_____
_____

2. The **EVIDENCE** to support what I **BELIEVE** is possible looks like this…

_____
_____
_____
_____

3. I was excited to **RECEIVE** (fill in the blank) last week…

_____
_____
_____
_____

ABUNDANCE IS A FEELING

Make a list of all the ways you felt or observed
ABUNDANCE in your life last week…

_____	_____
_____	_____
_____	_____
_____	_____
_____	_____
_____	_____
_____	_____
_____	_____
_____	_____
_____	_____
_____	_____
_____	_____
_____	_____
_____	_____

Date: ____ /____ /20____

WEEK 17

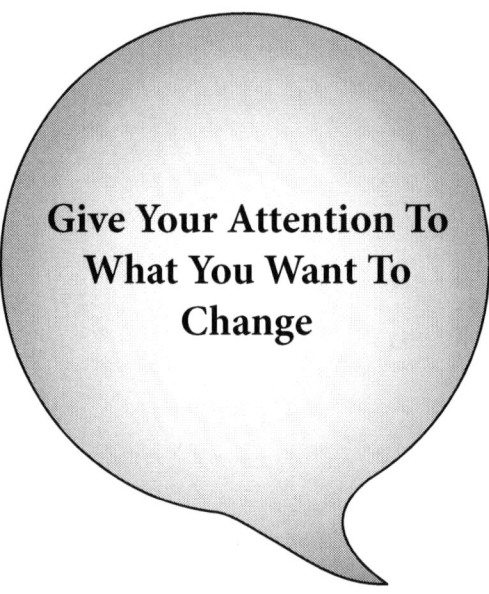

Give Your Attention To What You Want To Change

Most people want to live a happy and abundant life. What that looks like is different for every person on the planet.

If you find yourself wanting things to change in your personal life or make changes for the betterment of the planet, it all begins with you.

Put your attention on 'what' you want to change and not 'what's wrong' with your life or the planet.

Find ways to make a positive contribution 'for something' and not 'against' something. Focus on the positive changes you want.

1. My **INTENTION** for this week (around relationships, money, health, career and/or business) is …

_____
_____
_____
_____

2. Last week I felt **MOST GRATEFUL** for …

_____
_____
_____
_____

3. I **DELIBERATELY** used the Law of Attraction to attract…

_____
_____
_____
_____

4. I am **IN THE PROCESS** of manifesting…

_____
_____
_____
_____

5. I **FELT** major **POSITIVE VIBES** last week when …

_____
_____
_____
_____

THE
Ask ~ Believe ~ Receive
PROCESS

1. My **ASK** for this week is…

_____
_____
_____
_____

2. The **EVIDENCE** to support what I **BELIEVE** is possible looks like this…

_____
_____
_____
_____

3. I was excited to **RECEIVE** (fill in the blank) last week…

_____
_____
_____
_____

ABUNDANCE IS A FEELING

Make a list of all the ways you felt or observed
ABUNDANCE in your life last week…

_____   _____
_____   _____
_____   _____
_____   _____
_____   _____
_____   _____
_____   _____
_____   _____
_____   _____
_____   _____
_____   _____
_____   _____
_____   _____
_____   _____

WEEK 18

Wishing To Win The Lottery May Never Happen For You

If you are '*wishing*' that you will win the lottery, chances are that may never happen for you.

From a law of attraction perspective even though you 'think' you want to win, most people don't really 'believe' that they will win.

The way that will show up is by you knowing 'in your gut' that it's probably not going to happen for you.

However, when you do start to win even the smallest amount remember to 'celebrate the closeness of the match' to attract more.

1. My **INTENTION** for this week (around relationships, money, health, career and/or business) is ...

_____
_____
_____
_____

2. Last week I felt **MOST GRATEFUL** for ...

_____
_____
_____
_____

3. I **DELIBERATELY** used the Law of Attraction to attract...

_____
_____
_____
_____

4. I am **IN THE PROCESS** of manifesting...

_____
_____
_____
_____

5. I **FELT** major **POSITIVE VIBES** last week when ...

_____
_____
_____
_____

THE
Ask ~ Believe ~ Receive
PROCESS

1. My **ASK** for this week is…

   _____
   _____
   _____
   _____

2. The **EVIDENCE** to support what I **BELIEVE** is possible looks like this…

   _____
   _____
   _____
   _____

3. I was excited to **RECEIVE** (fill in the blank) last week…

   _____
   _____
   _____
   _____

ABUNDANCE IS A FEELING

Make a list of all the ways you felt or observed
ABUNDANCE in your life last week…

_____	_____
_____	_____
_____	_____
_____	_____
_____	_____
_____	_____
_____	_____
_____	_____
_____	_____
_____	_____
_____	_____
_____	_____
_____	_____
_____	_____
_____	_____

Date: ___/___/20___

WEEK 19

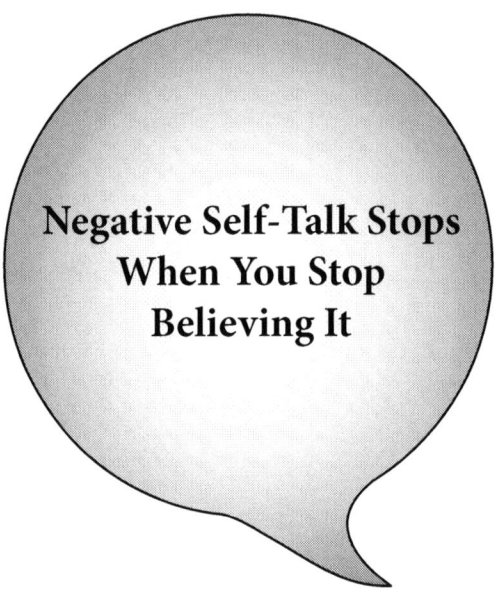

Negative Self-Talk Stops When You Stop Believing It

Your limiting beliefs start right from birth until the age of 6. You can spend the rest of your life trying to validate those negative, self-defeating, self-talk thoughts.

The moment *you become aware* that you have negative self-talk going on, you have taken the first step in bringing about change. Examine that thought – is it really true about you or does someone want you to believe it's true?

Use the phrase 'I am in the process of…' filled with more positive-serving thoughts that make you feel good.

1. My **INTENTION** for this week (around relationships, money, health, career and/or business) is …

_____
_____
_____
_____

2. Last week I felt **MOST GRATEFUL** for …

_____
_____
_____
_____

3. I **DELIBERATELY** used the Law of Attraction to attract…

_____
_____
_____
_____

4. I am **IN THE PROCESS** of manifesting…

_____
_____
_____
_____

5. I **FELT** major **POSITIVE VIBES** last week when …

_____
_____
_____
_____

THE
Ask ~ Believe ~ Receive
PROCESS

1. My **ASK** for this week is…

   _____
   _____
   _____
   _____

2. The **EVIDENCE** to support what I **BELIEVE** is possible looks like this…

   _____
   _____
   _____
   _____

3. I was excited to **RECEIVE** (fill in the blank) last week…

   _____
   _____
   _____
   _____

ABUNDANCE IS A FEELING

Make a list of all the ways you felt or observed
ABUNDANCE in your life last week…

Date: ____ /____ /20____

WEEK 20

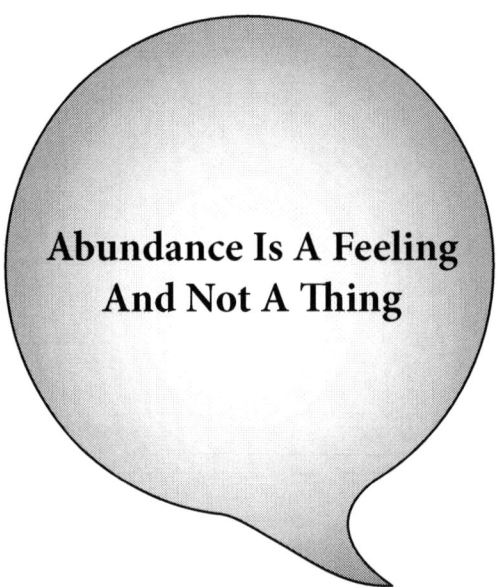

Abundance Is A Feeling And Not A Thing

Do you find yourself saying that you *don't have enough*…(fill in the blank)? If so, you are coming from a lack consciousness and every time you use that phrase, you attract more of what you already don't have enough of!

Many people think that 'money' is what being abundant means. It may be so, but the bigger truth is that …

> Abundance is a feeling

Look around you and notice what makes you feel great. Being in nature is one of the best ways to recognize and feel abundant.

1. My **INTENTION** for this week (around relationships, money, health, career and/or business) is …

_____
_____
_____
_____

2. Last week I felt **MOST GRATEFUL** for …

_____
_____
_____
_____

3. I **DELIBERATELY** used the Law of Attraction to attract…

_____
_____
_____
_____

4. I am **IN THE PROCESS** of manifesting…

_____
_____
_____
_____

5. I **FELT** major **POSITIVE VIBES** last week when …

_____
_____
_____
_____

THE
Ask ~ Believe ~ Receive
PROCESS

1. My **ASK** for this week is…

_____
_____
_____
_____

2. The **EVIDENCE** to support what I **BELIEVE** is possible looks like this…

_____
_____
_____
_____

3. I was excited to **RECEIVE** (fill in the blank) last week…

_____
_____
_____
_____

ABUNDANCE IS A FEELING

Make a list of all the ways you felt or observed
ABUNDANCE in your life last week…

Date: ____ /____ /20____

WEEK 21

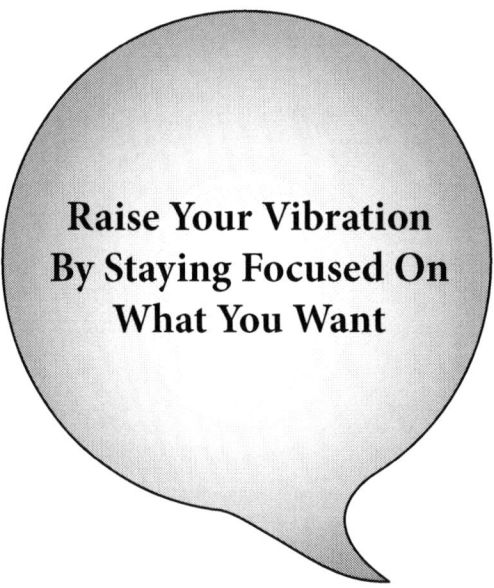

Raise Your Vibration By Staying Focused On What You Want

You know that having crystal clear clarity about 'what you want' is one of the keys to manifesting. Another key to manifesting is 'how you feel' about what you want. Ask yourself …

> What will it feel like when I
> have what I desire?

Look for evidence by observing other people who have what you want. Let go of any negative feelings, such as jealousy, when you see others have what you want. Instead focus on the positive vibrations about *how you will feel* when you have that.

1. My **INTENTION** for this week (around relationships, money, health, career and/or business) is …

_____
_____
_____
_____

2. Last week I felt **MOST GRATEFUL** for …

_____
_____
_____
_____

3. I **DELIBERATELY** used the Law of Attraction to attract…

_____
_____
_____
_____

4. I am **IN THE PROCESS** of manifesting…

_____
_____
_____
_____

5. I **FELT** major **POSITIVE VIBES** last week when …

_____
_____
_____
_____

THE
Ask ~ Believe ~ Receive
PROCESS

1. My **ASK** for this week is…

_____
_____
_____
_____

2. The **EVIDENCE** to support what I **BELIEVE** is possible looks like this…

_____
_____
_____
_____

3. I was excited to **RECEIVE** (fill in the blank) last week…

_____
_____
_____
_____

ABUNDANCE IS A FEELING

Make a list of all the ways you felt or observed
ABUNDANCE in your life last week…

_____ _____
_____ _____
_____ _____
_____ _____
_____ _____
_____ _____
_____ _____
_____ _____
_____ _____
_____ _____
_____ _____
_____ _____
_____ _____
_____ _____
_____ _____

Date: ____ / ____ /20____

WEEK 22

Imagine that you have an invisible bubble all around you and that every thought you think or say – is in this bubble.

In law of attraction we call this your …

> Vibrational Bubble

Since you know that every thought has either positive or negative energy around it, and you know that like energy attracts more like energy, would it make sense to be more mindful of what you put in your vibrational bubble?

Whatever you are watching or listening to, it goes in the bubble.

1. My **INTENTION** for this week (around relationships, money, health, career and/or business) is …

_____
_____
_____
_____

2. Last week I felt **MOST GRATEFUL** for …

_____
_____
_____
_____

3. I **DELIBERATELY** used the Law of Attraction to attract…

_____
_____
_____
_____

4. I am **IN THE PROCESS** of manifesting…

_____
_____
_____
_____

5. I **FELT** major **POSITIVE VIBES** last week when …

_____
_____
_____
_____

THE
Ask ~ Believe ~ Receive
PROCESS

1. My **ASK** for this week is…

_____
_____
_____
_____

2. The **EVIDENCE** to support what I **BELIEVE** is possible looks like this…

_____
_____
_____
_____

3. I was excited to **RECEIVE** (fill in the blank) last week…

_____
_____
_____
_____

ABUNDANCE IS A FEELING

Make a list of all the ways you felt or observed
ABUNDANCE in your life last week…

_____   _____
_____   _____
_____   _____
_____   _____
_____   _____
_____   _____
_____   _____
_____   _____
_____   _____
_____   _____
_____   _____
_____   _____
_____   _____
_____   _____

Date: ____ /____ /20____

WEEK 23

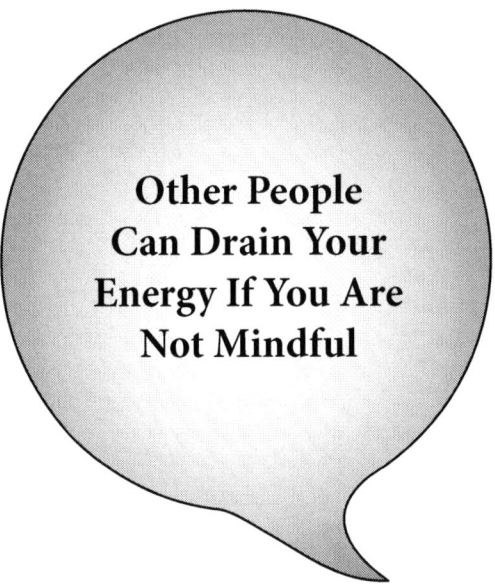

Other People Can Drain Your Energy If You Are Not Mindful

Do you have any energy draining vampires in your life? You know them. They most often feel great after talking with you and you end up feeling depressed!

Since the law of attraction is obedient, *it will continue to help you attract the energy draining vampires until you say "No more!"* If it's someone you can't avoid seeing then set a time limit on how much of your time they can have.

Be mindful – it's your life and your time that you are giving to someone else.

1. My **INTENTION** for this week (around relationships, money, health, career and/or business) is ...

_____
_____
_____
_____

2. Last week I felt **MOST GRATEFUL** for ...

_____
_____
_____
_____

3. I **DELIBERATELY** used the Law of Attraction to attract...

_____
_____
_____
_____

4. I am **IN THE PROCESS** of manifesting...

_____
_____
_____
_____

5. I **FELT** major **POSITIVE VIBES** last week when ...

_____
_____
_____
_____

THE
Ask ~ Believe ~ Receive
PROCESS

1. My **ASK** for this week is…

_____
_____
_____
_____

2. The **EVIDENCE** to support what I **BELIEVE** is possible looks like this…

_____
_____
_____
_____

3. I was excited to **RECEIVE** (fill in the blank) last week…

_____
_____
_____
_____

ABUNDANCE IS A FEELING

Make a list of all the ways you felt or observed
ABUNDANCE in your life last week…

_____   _____

_____   _____

_____   _____

_____   _____

_____   _____

_____   _____

_____   _____

_____   _____

_____   _____

_____   _____

_____   _____

_____   _____

_____   _____

_____   _____

Date: ____ /____ /20____

WEEK 24

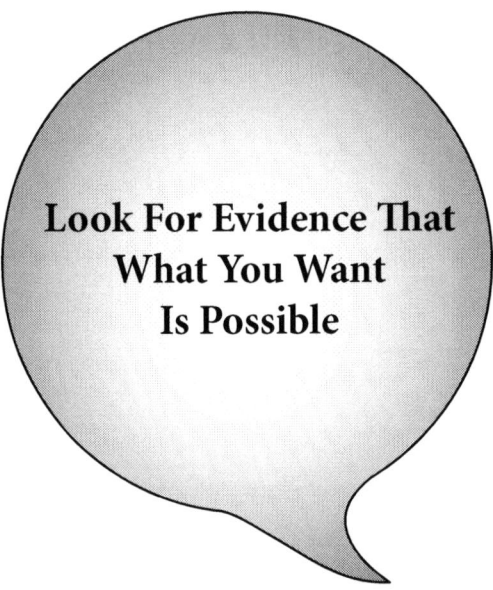

Look For Evidence That What You Want Is Possible

Once you have decided what it is you want, one of the key ways to attract more, is by looking for evidence.

>Look for evidence everywhere

The evidence you find does not have to be perfect. It just needs to give you enough evidence that what you want is possible.

If you see someone who has what you want, rejoice in that. Put yourself in that vibration of what that will feel like.

Stay focused on what you want and believe that it is possible for you.

1. My **INTENTION** for this week (around relationships, money, health, career and/or business) is …

_____
_____
_____
_____

2. Last week I felt **MOST GRATEFUL** for …

_____
_____
_____
_____

3. I **DELIBERATELY** used the Law of Attraction to attract…

_____
_____
_____
_____

4. I am **IN THE PROCESS** of manifesting…

_____
_____
_____
_____

5. I **FELT** major **POSITIVE VIBES** last week when …

_____
_____
_____
_____

THE
Ask ~ Believe ~ Receive
PROCESS

1. My **ASK** for this week is…

2. The **EVIDENCE** to support what I **BELIEVE** is possible looks like this…

3. I was excited to **RECEIVE** (fill in the blank) last week…

ABUNDANCE IS A FEELING

Make a list of all the ways you felt or observed
ABUNDANCE in your life last week…

_____   _____
_____   _____
_____   _____
_____   _____
_____   _____
_____   _____
_____   _____
_____   _____
_____   _____
_____   _____
_____   _____
_____   _____
_____   _____
_____   _____
_____   _____

Date: ___ / ___ /20___

WEEK 25

As much as someone else may tell you that you are responsible for their happiness, or lack of it, this is simply not true.

You can only be responsible for your own emotions and vibrations whether they are positive or negative.

It doesn't mean that your vibrations don't affect someone else, they do, but how they are received is not your responsibility.

Being responsible means 'being able to respond'. How you respond in any situation is an individual choice and only you can make that for yourself.

1. My **INTENTION** for this week (around relationships, money, health, career and/or business) is …

_____
_____
_____
_____

2. Last week I felt **MOST GRATEFUL** for …

_____
_____
_____
_____

3. I **DELIBERATELY** used the Law of Attraction to attract…

_____
_____
_____
_____

4. I am **IN THE PROCESS** of manifesting…

_____
_____
_____
_____

5. I **FELT** major **POSITIVE VIBES** last week when …

_____
_____
_____
_____

THE
Ask ~ Believe ~ Receive
PROCESS

1. My **ASK** for this week is…

   _____
   _____
   _____
   _____

2. The **EVIDENCE** to support what I **BELIEVE** is possible looks like this…

   _____
   _____
   _____
   _____

3. I was excited to **RECEIVE** (fill in the blank) last week…

   _____
   _____
   _____
   _____

ABUNDANCE IS A FEELING

Make a list of all the ways you felt or observed
ABUNDANCE in your life last week…

_____   _____
_____   _____
_____   _____
_____   _____
_____   _____
_____   _____
_____   _____
_____   _____
_____   _____
_____   _____
_____   _____
_____   _____
_____   _____
_____   _____

Date: ____ /____ /20____

WEEK 26

Have an Attitude of Gratitude

You've heard this statement many times over your lifetime and the reason you hear it so often is because it has a huge impact on this planet.

When you have that ...

> Attitude of Gratitude

you are emitting a positive vibration. Every positive vibration attracts another positive vibration and on and on it goes – around the world.

Now that you are becoming a 'deliberate attractor' you know how powerful you really are. People will notice this about you and be attracted to you because of this attitude of gratitude.

1. My **INTENTION** for this week (around relationships, money, health, career and/or business) is …

_____
_____
_____
_____

2. Last week I felt **MOST GRATEFUL** for …

_____
_____
_____
_____

3. I **DELIBERATELY** used the Law of Attraction to attract…

_____
_____
_____
_____

4. I am **IN THE PROCESS** of manifesting…

_____
_____
_____
_____

5. I **FELT** major **POSITIVE VIBES** last week when …

_____
_____
_____
_____

THE
Ask ~ Believe ~ Receive
PROCESS

1. My **ASK** for this week is…

2. The **EVIDENCE** to support what I **BELIEVE** is possible looks like this…

3. I was excited to **RECEIVE** (fill in the blank) last week…

ABUNDANCE IS A FEELING

Make a list of all the ways you felt or observed
ABUNDANCE in your life last week…

_____   _____
_____   _____
_____   _____
_____   _____
_____   _____
_____   _____
_____   _____
_____   _____
_____   _____
_____   _____
_____   _____
_____   _____
_____   _____
_____   _____

Date: ____ /____ /20____

WEEK 27

In a previous law of attraction weekly tip, you learned the importance of avoiding the words 'Don't Not No'.

There are times when 'no' may be the right word but you can find another way to reframe your 'no' response to make it more positive.

If you wanted to say "no thanks" to something or someone you just need to *tell them what you do want*. For example, you could say 'I prefer this or I prefer that' and they get the message.

1. My **INTENTION** for this week (around relationships, money, health, career and/or business) is …

2. Last week I felt **MOST GRATEFUL** for …

3. I **DELIBERATELY** used the Law of Attraction to attract…

4. I am **IN THE PROCESS** of manifesting…

5. I **FELT** major **POSITIVE VIBES** last week when …

THE
Ask ~ Believe ~ Receive
PROCESS

1. My **ASK** for this week is…

2. The **EVIDENCE** to support what I **BELIEVE** is possible looks like this…

3. I was excited to **RECEIVE** (fill in the blank) last week…

ABUNDANCE IS A FEELING

Make a list of all the ways you felt or observed
ABUNDANCE in your life last week…

Date: ____ / ____ /20____

WEEK 28

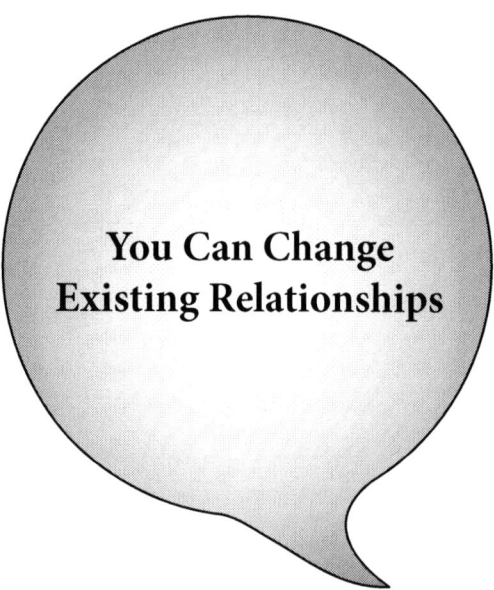

You Can Change Existing Relationships

If you find yourself in a relationship where you want things to change, you have the power to do that. You have to decide what you want to change and what your role and responsiblities are in the relationship.

You may need to create your 'Don't Want' list and your 'Do Want' list, and have your partner do the same. Find out where you connect and where the differences lie.

Only you can decide what you want to change in yourself to make the relationship better for yourself.

1. My **INTENTION** for this week (around relationships, money, health, career and/or business) is …

2. Last week I felt **MOST GRATEFUL** for …

3. I **DELIBERATELY** used the Law of Attraction to attract…

4. I am **IN THE PROCESS** of manifesting…

5. I **FELT** major **POSITIVE VIBES** last week when …

THE
Ask ~ Believe ~ Receive
PROCESS

1. My **ASK** for this week is…

   _____
   _____
   _____
   _____

2. The **EVIDENCE** to support what I **BELIEVE** is possible looks like this…

   _____
   _____
   _____
   _____

3. I was excited to **RECEIVE** (fill in the blank) last week…

   _____
   _____
   _____
   _____

ABUNDANCE IS A FEELING

Make a list of all the ways you felt or observed
ABUNDANCE in your life last week…

Date: ____ /____ /20____

WEEK 29

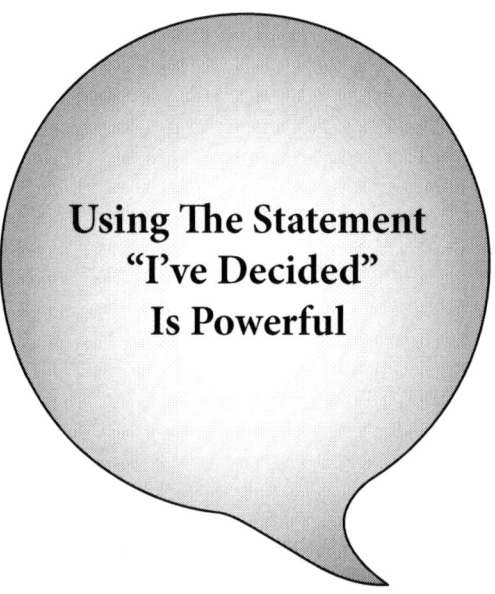

One of the most powerful thoughts you can have is when you use this statement…

I've decided

The law of attraction loves this kind of positive, assertive energy and will bring you more of it.

Once you are crystal clear on your decision about something, you will get the support you need to make it your reality.

When you make a decision it often involves change. Stay focused on how you will feel once this change occurs regardless if others are trying to talk you out of it.

1. My **INTENTION** for this week (around relationships, money, health, career and/or business) is …

_____
_____
_____
_____

2. Last week I felt **MOST GRATEFUL** for …

_____
_____
_____
_____

3. I **DELIBERATELY** used the Law of Attraction to attract…

_____
_____
_____
_____

4. I am **IN THE PROCESS** of manifesting…

_____
_____
_____
_____

5. I **FELT** major **POSITIVE VIBES** last week when …

_____
_____
_____
_____

THE
Ask ~ Believe ~ Receive
PROCESS

1. My **ASK** for this week is…

_____
_____
_____
_____

2. The **EVIDENCE** to support what I **BELIEVE** is possible looks like this…

_____
_____
_____
_____

3. I was excited to **RECEIVE** (fill in the blank) last week…

_____
_____
_____
_____

ABUNDANCE IS A FEELING

Make a list of all the ways you felt or observed
ABUNDANCE in your life last week…

_____   _____
_____   _____
_____   _____
_____   _____
_____   _____
_____   _____
_____   _____
_____   _____
_____   _____
_____   _____
_____   _____
_____   _____
_____   _____
_____   _____
_____   _____
_____   _____

WEEK 30

It's Better To Release Weight Than To Lose It

You might be someone who wants to be slimmer or healthier by losing some weight.

From a law of attraction perspective before you start any diet or eating-habit lifestyle changes, *change the word 'lose' to 'release'*.

The reason for this small mindset shift is because if you tell your subconscious you have lost weight it will try and find it for you and give it back to you.

Focus on exercise and healthy foods and how you will feel once you have released the weight.

1. My **INTENTION** for this week (around relationships, money, health, career and/or business) is …

_____
_____
_____
_____

2. Last week I felt **MOST GRATEFUL** for …

_____
_____
_____
_____

3. I **DELIBERATELY** used the Law of Attraction to attract…

_____
_____
_____
_____

4. I am **IN THE PROCESS** of manifesting…

_____
_____
_____
_____

5. I **FELT** major **POSITIVE VIBES** last week when …

_____
_____
_____
_____

THE
Ask ~ Believe ~ Receive
PROCESS

1. My **ASK** for this week is…

_____
_____
_____
_____

2. The **EVIDENCE** to support what I **BELIEVE** is possible looks like this…

_____
_____
_____
_____

3. I was excited to **RECEIVE** (fill in the blank) last week…

_____
_____
_____
_____

ABUNDANCE IS A FEELING

Make a list of all the ways you felt or observed
ABUNDANCE in your life last week…

Date: ____ /____ /20____

WEEK 31

Being Selfish Is Just Good Self-Care

I think moms in general struggle with taking good self-care because they typically put their family first.

Whether you are a mom or not, it is good and necessary that you *take good care of your 'self'*.

The law of attraction wants you to be happy and healthy and you cannot be this way if your mindset is telling you that this is a negative and not-nice quality to have.

It is esssential to you feeling good so please, be selfish, do things for yourself.

1. My **INTENTION** for this week (around relationships, money, health, career and/or business) is …

2. Last week I felt **MOST GRATEFUL** for …

3. I **DELIBERATELY** used the Law of Attraction to attract…

4. I am **IN THE PROCESS** of manifesting…

5. I **FELT** major **POSITIVE VIBES** last week when …

THE
Ask ~ Believe ~ Receive
PROCESS

1. My **ASK** for this week is…

   _____
   _____
   _____
   _____

2. The **EVIDENCE** to support what I **BELIEVE** is possible looks like this…

   _____
   _____
   _____
   _____

3. I was excited to **RECEIVE** (fill in the blank) last week…

   _____
   _____
   _____
   _____

ABUNDANCE IS A FEELING

Make a list of all the ways you felt or observed
ABUNDANCE in your life last week…

_____	_____
_____	_____
_____	_____
_____	_____
_____	_____
_____	_____
_____	_____
_____	_____
_____	_____
_____	_____
_____	_____
_____	_____
_____	_____
_____	_____
_____	_____

Date: ____ /____ /20____

WEEK 32

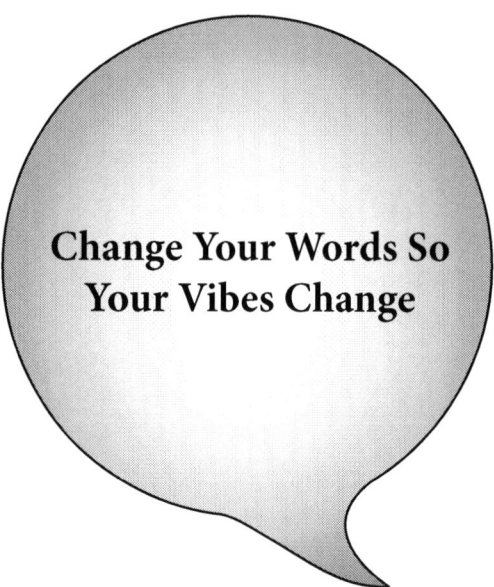

Change Your Words So Your Vibes Change

Words words words. You may have never realized just how important every word is that you say or think.

Every word or thought emits a vibration and that vibe can have a a greater impact than the words or thoughts themselves.

When you are using negative words you are also sending off a negative vibration. Conversely when you use positive language you send a positive vibe.

So, you need to be mindful of the words you use and chose the ones that send the vibe you want.

1. My **INTENTION** for this week (around relationships, money, health, career and/or business) is …

_____
_____
_____
_____

2. Last week I felt **MOST GRATEFUL** for …

_____
_____
_____
_____

3. I **DELIBERATELY** used the Law of Attraction to attract…

_____
_____
_____
_____

4. I am **IN THE PROCESS** of manifesting…

_____
_____
_____
_____

5. I **FELT** major **POSITIVE VIBES** last week when …

_____
_____
_____
_____

THE
Ask ~ Believe ~ Receive
PROCESS

1. My **ASK** for this week is…

_____
_____
_____
_____

2. The **EVIDENCE** to support what I **BELIEVE** is possible looks like this…

_____
_____
_____
_____

3. I was excited to **RECEIVE** (fill in the blank) last week…

_____
_____
_____
_____

ABUNDANCE IS A FEELING

Make a list of all the ways you felt or observed
ABUNDANCE in your life last week…

WEEK 33

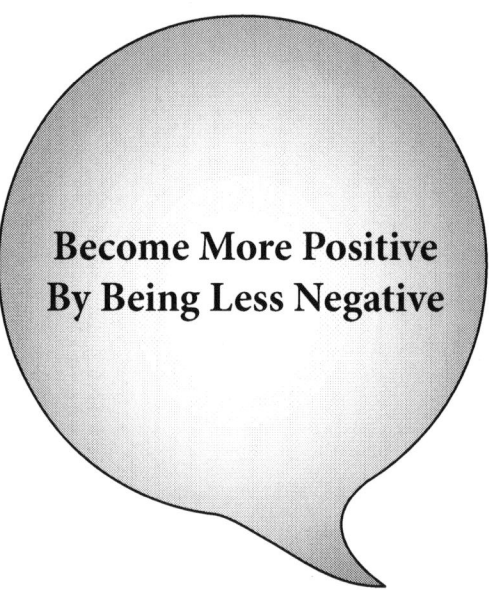

Become More Positive By Being Less Negative

You may find yourself attracting negative people, things or circumstances and wonder why that is happening.

It's happening because you are *focusing on* the negative people, things or circumstances *instead of* looking for more positive people, things or circumstances to attract into your life.

When you notice you are going down a road of negativity - STOP. Reset your direction and set a new intention to find ways to be more positive.

This slight mindset shift will allow the law of attraction to match the new vibrations.

1. My **INTENTION** for this week (around relationships, money, health, career and/or business) is ...

2. Last week I felt **MOST GRATEFUL** for ...

3. I **DELIBERATELY** used the Law of Attraction to attract...

4. I am **IN THE PROCESS** of manifesting...

5. I **FELT** major **POSITIVE VIBES** last week when ...

THE
Ask ~ Believe ~ Receive
PROCESS

1. My **ASK** for this week is…

   _____
   _____
   _____
   _____

2. The **EVIDENCE** to support what I **BELIEVE** is possible looks like this…

   _____
   _____
   _____
   _____

3. I was excited to **RECEIVE** (fill in the blank) last week…

   _____
   _____
   _____
   _____

ABUNDANCE IS A FEELING

Make a list of all the ways you felt or observed
ABUNDANCE in your life last week…

_____	_____
_____	_____
_____	_____
_____	_____
_____	_____
_____	_____
_____	_____
_____	_____
_____	_____
_____	_____
_____	_____
_____	_____
_____	_____
_____	_____

Date: ____ /____ /20____

WEEK 34

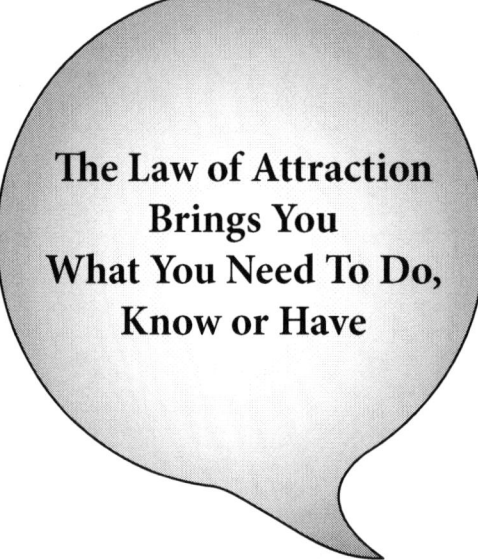

The Law of Attraction Brings You What You Need To Do, Know or Have

In order to deliberately manifest you need to go through the 3 Step 'Ask Believe Receive' process.

And, for the law of attraction to assist you in attracting what you want, you need to remove as much doubt as possible.

Once you have done that and you are ready to receive, *the law of attraction will bring you what you need to do, know or have.*

You may need to meet someone, learn something or get something, to support your manifesting. Express gratitude for whatever comes your way.

1. My **INTENTION** for this week (around relationships, money, health, career and/or business) is …

2. Last week I felt **MOST GRATEFUL** for …

3. I **DELIBERATELY** used the Law of Attraction to attract…

4. I am **IN THE PROCESS** of manifesting…

5. I **FELT** major **POSITIVE VIBES** last week when …

THE
Ask ~ Believe ~ Receive
PROCESS

1. My **ASK** for this week is…

_____
_____
_____
_____

2. The **EVIDENCE** to support what I **BELIEVE** is possible looks like this…

_____
_____
_____
_____

3. I was excited to **RECEIVE** (fill in the blank) last week…

_____
_____
_____
_____

ABUNDANCE IS A FEELING

Make a list of all the ways you felt or observed
ABUNDANCE in your life last week…

Date: ____ /____ /20____

WEEK 35

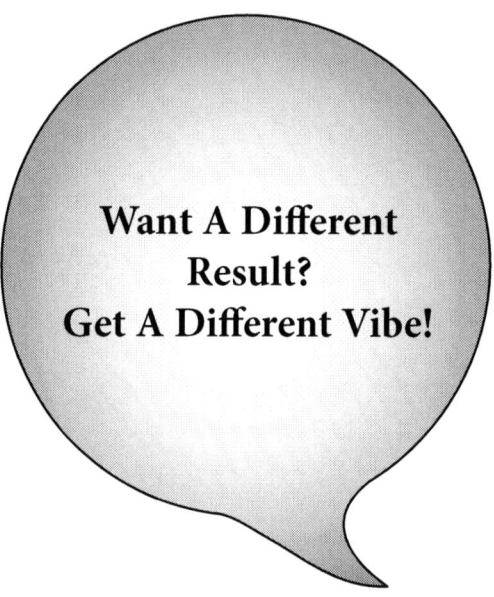

Want A Different Result? Get A Different Vibe!

If you have been using the 'Words=Results' relationship formula you know how important your words are.

However, what you may not know is that how you *FEEL* about what you say or think is what is the real driving force behind you attracting what you want.

It's the negative or positive vibration that you are giving off around the words and thoughts you have about the result you want – that matters most.

The expression 'Whether you think you can or can't – you're right!' is pure law of attraction!

1. My **INTENTION** for this week (around relationships, money, health, career and/or business) is …

2. Last week I felt **MOST GRATEFUL** for …

3. I **DELIBERATELY** used the Law of Attraction to attract…

4. I am **IN THE PROCESS** of manifesting…

5. I **FELT** major **POSITIVE VIBES** last week when …

THE
Ask ~ Believe ~ Receive
PROCESS

1. My **ASK** for this week is…

_____
_____
_____
_____

2. The **EVIDENCE** to support what I **BELIEVE** is possible looks like this…

_____
_____
_____
_____

3. I was excited to **RECEIVE** (fill in the blank) last week…

_____
_____
_____
_____

ABUNDANCE IS A FEELING

Make a list of all the ways you felt or observed
ABUNDANCE in your life last week…

_____   _____
_____   _____
_____   _____
_____   _____
_____   _____
_____   _____
_____   _____
_____   _____
_____   _____
_____   _____
_____   _____
_____   _____
_____   _____
_____   _____

Date: ____ / ____ /20____

WEEK 36

Vision Boards Work When You Believe They Do

Visualizing what you desire has been a proven technique to manifesting. It's like being able to run the movie all the way through so you have a good idea of what the end result will look like.

If you *love the idea of creating a Vision Board* and you believe this helps you manifest, then do it.

If, however, the very idea drains your energy you need to find another way to visualize. Take photos, create a video, create your own app on your phone, buy books, write in your journal – do whatever feels good to you.

1. My **INTENTION** for this week (around relationships, money, health, career and/or business) is ...

_____
_____
_____
_____

2. Last week I felt **MOST GRATEFUL** for ...

_____
_____
_____
_____

3. I **DELIBERATELY** used the Law of Attraction to attract...

_____
_____
_____
_____

4. I am **IN THE PROCESS** of manifesting...

_____
_____
_____
_____

5. I **FELT** major **POSITIVE VIBES** last week when ...

_____
_____
_____
_____

THE
Ask ~ Believe ~ Receive
PROCESS

1. My **ASK** for this week is…

_____
_____
_____
_____

2. The **EVIDENCE** to support what I **BELIEVE** is possible looks like this…

_____
_____
_____
_____

3. I was excited to **RECEIVE** (fill in the blank) last week…

_____
_____
_____
_____

ABUNDANCE IS A FEELING

Make a list of all the ways you felt or observed
ABUNDANCE in your life last week…

WEEK 37

A Vibrational Business Plan Works

You may be unfamiliar with a Vibrational Business Plan but it's a great law of attraction tool versus the more common business plan.

A Vibrational Business Plan can be done on bristol board or on your computer. Create it so you can look at it daily.

Make 3 rows at the top with these headings:

1) *What I Know For Sure*
2) *What I Am Giving My Attention To*
3) *Room For More*

Underneath each heading write your desires. As they manifest move them up.

1. My **INTENTION** for this week (around relationships, money, health, career and/or business) is …

_____

_____

_____

_____

2. Last week I felt **MOST GRATEFUL** for …

_____

_____

_____

_____

3. I **DELIBERATELY** used the Law of Attraction to attract…

_____

_____

_____

_____

4. I am **IN THE PROCESS** of manifesting…

_____

_____

_____

_____

5. I **FELT** major **POSITIVE VIBES** last week when …

_____

_____

_____

_____

THE
Ask ~ Believe ~ Receive
PROCESS

1. My **ASK** for this week is…

_____
_____
_____
_____

2. The **EVIDENCE** to support what I **BELIEVE** is possible looks like this…

_____
_____
_____
_____

3. I was excited to **RECEIVE** (fill in the blank) last week…

_____
_____
_____
_____

ABUNDANCE IS A FEELING

Make a list of all the ways you felt or observed
ABUNDANCE in your life last week…

_____	_____
_____	_____
_____	_____
_____	_____
_____	_____
_____	_____
_____	_____
_____	_____
_____	_____
_____	_____
_____	_____
_____	_____
_____	_____
_____	_____

Date: ____ / ____ /20____

WEEK 38

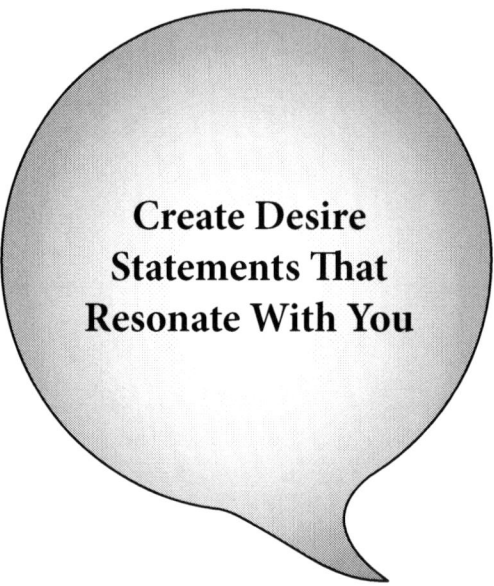

Create Desire Statements That Resonate With You

When you are working with the 'Ask Believe Receive' process a good way to reinforce your beliefs is to write *Desire Statements*. They must resonate with you in a good way.

If you want…

- Better Health
  "I love how it feels when I am playing with my children."

- More Abundance
  "I get so excited talking about going on our winter vacation."

- Better Relationships
  "Just thinking about having a partner is so awesome."

- Better Career
  "It feels so great to hear that other people respect my work."

1. My **INTENTION** for this week (around relationships, money, health, career and/or business) is …

_____
_____
_____
_____

2. Last week I felt **MOST GRATEFUL** for …

_____
_____
_____
_____

3. I **DELIBERATELY** used the Law of Attraction to attract…

_____
_____
_____
_____

4. I am **IN THE PROCESS** of manifesting…

_____
_____
_____
_____

5. I **FELT** major **POSITIVE VIBES** last week when …

_____
_____
_____
_____

THE
Ask ~ Believe ~ Receive
PROCESS

1. My **ASK** for this week is…

   _____
   _____
   _____
   _____

2. The **EVIDENCE** to support what I **BELIEVE** is possible looks like this…

   _____
   _____
   _____
   _____

3. I was excited to **RECEIVE** (fill in the blank) last week…

   _____
   _____
   _____
   _____

ABUNDANCE IS A FEELING

Make a list of all the ways you felt or observed
ABUNDANCE in your life last week…

_____	_____
_____	_____
_____	_____
_____	_____
_____	_____
_____	_____
_____	_____
_____	_____
_____	_____
_____	_____
_____	_____
_____	_____
_____	_____
_____	_____
_____	_____
_____	_____

Date: ____ / ____ /20____

WEEK 39

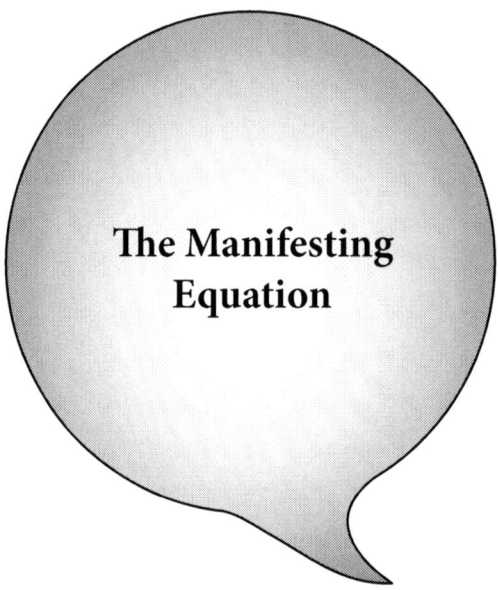

The Manifesting Equation

From a law of attraction perspective to 'allow' means that you need to remove as much doubt as possible to attract.

There is an equation that states:

The *more doubt* you have about your ability to manifest your desire, the less *likely* you are to get what you want.

If you have some *doubt* it is possible that *you will manifest* but that may take some time.

And if you have *no doubt* whatsoever and a *strong desire* for something then you are *most likely to manifest*.

1. My **INTENTION** for this week (around relationships, money, health, career and/or business) is …

2. Last week I felt **MOST GRATEFUL** for …

3. I **DELIBERATELY** used the Law of Attraction to attract…

4. I am **IN THE PROCESS** of manifesting…

5. I **FELT** major **POSITIVE VIBES** last week when …

THE
Ask ~ Believe ~ Receive
PROCESS

1. My **ASK** for this week is…

   _____
   _____
   _____
   _____

2. The **EVIDENCE** to support what I **BELIEVE** is possible looks like this…

   _____
   _____
   _____
   _____

3. I was excited to **RECEIVE** (fill in the blank) last week…

   _____
   _____
   _____
   _____

ABUNDANCE IS A FEELING

Make a list of all the ways you felt or observed
ABUNDANCE in your life last week…

WEEK 40

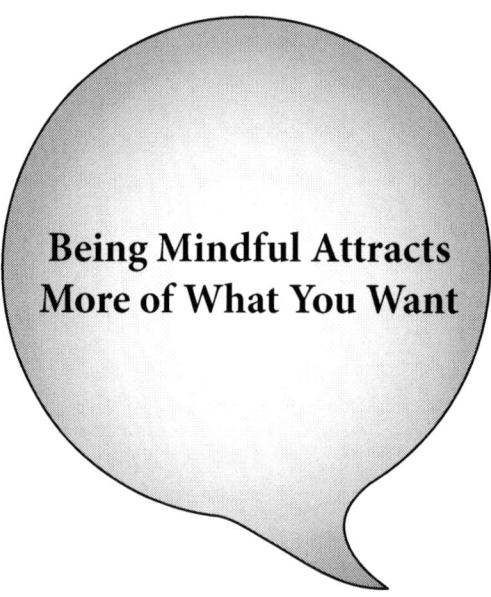

Being Mindful Attracts More of What You Want

When you set your intention about something, you are being specific about what you intend to happen. This is a form of 'mindfulness'.

Being mindful also requires *intentional action* to attract what you want.

You only take intentional action when it *feels right* for you. If it doesn't feel right, you give off negative vibes. Your being mindful of this is also going to help the manifestation process.

Give the law of attraction time to set things in motion or you may slow down or debunk the process.

1. My **INTENTION** for this week (around relationships, money, health, career and/or business) is …

_____
_____
_____
_____

2. Last week I felt **MOST GRATEFUL** for …

_____
_____
_____
_____

3. I **DELIBERATELY** used the Law of Attraction to attract…

_____
_____
_____
_____

4. I am **IN THE PROCESS** of manifesting…

_____
_____
_____
_____

5. I **FELT** major **POSITIVE VIBES** last week when …

_____
_____
_____
_____

THE
Ask ~ Believe ~ Receive
PROCESS

1. My **ASK** for this week is…

   _____
   _____
   _____
   _____

2. The **EVIDENCE** to support what I **BELIEVE** is possible looks like this…

   _____
   _____
   _____
   _____

3. I was excited to **RECEIVE** (fill in the blank) last week…

   _____
   _____
   _____
   _____

ABUNDANCE IS A FEELING

Make a list of all the ways you felt or observed
ABUNDANCE in your life last week…

Date: ____ /____ /20____

WEEK 41

Look At All Your Law of Attraction Receipts

The more deliberately you use the law of attraction, the more you put the tools and principles to work in your daily life, the more success you will have manifesting.

And as you manifest it's good practice to take a good look at all of the '*receipts*' you have from your manifesting.

A receipt is anything that represents your success in manifesting. It could be a monetary receipt, or, it can be anything that gives you *proof or evidence* of your ability to manifest.

1. My **INTENTION** for this week (around relationships, money, health, career and/or business) is …

2. Last week I felt **MOST GRATEFUL** for …

3. I **DELIBERATELY** used the Law of Attraction to attract…

4. I am **IN THE PROCESS** of manifesting…

5. I **FELT** major **POSITIVE VIBES** last week when …

THE
Ask ~ Believe ~ Receive
PROCESS

1. My **ASK** for this week is…

   _____
   _____
   _____
   _____

2. The **EVIDENCE** to support what I **BELIEVE** is possible looks like this…

   _____
   _____
   _____
   _____

3. I was excited to **RECEIVE** (fill in the blank) last week…

   _____
   _____
   _____
   _____

ABUNDANCE IS A FEELING

Make a list of all the ways you felt or observed
ABUNDANCE in your life last week…

_____   _____
_____   _____
_____   _____
_____   _____
_____   _____
_____   _____
_____   _____
_____   _____
_____   _____
_____   _____
_____   _____
_____   _____
_____   _____
_____   _____
_____   _____
_____   _____

Date: ____ /____ /20____

WEEK 42

Celebrate The Closeness Of The Match

One of the techniques you can use when you are manifesting is to *celebrate the closeness of the match.*

What this means is that as soon as you notice the law of attraction is bringing something, anything to you related to your desire - you need to celebrate that.

The smallest thing that you attract needs to be acknowledged so you can continue to attract more.

Express gratitude for it and your positive vibrations will continue to attract more and eventually bring you your desire.

1. My **INTENTION** for this week (around relationships, money, health, career and/or business) is …

2. Last week I felt **MOST GRATEFUL** for …

3. I **DELIBERATELY** used the Law of Attraction to attract…

4. I am **IN THE PROCESS** of manifesting…

5. I **FELT** major **POSITIVE VIBES** last week when …

THE
Ask ~ Believe ~ Receive
PROCESS

1. My **ASK** for this week is…

_____
_____
_____
_____

2. The **EVIDENCE** to support what I **BELIEVE** is possible looks like this…

_____
_____
_____
_____

3. I was excited to **RECEIVE** (fill in the blank) last week…

_____
_____
_____
_____

ABUNDANCE IS A FEELING

Make a list of all the ways you felt or observed
ABUNDANCE in your life last week…

Date: ____ /____ /20____

WEEK 43

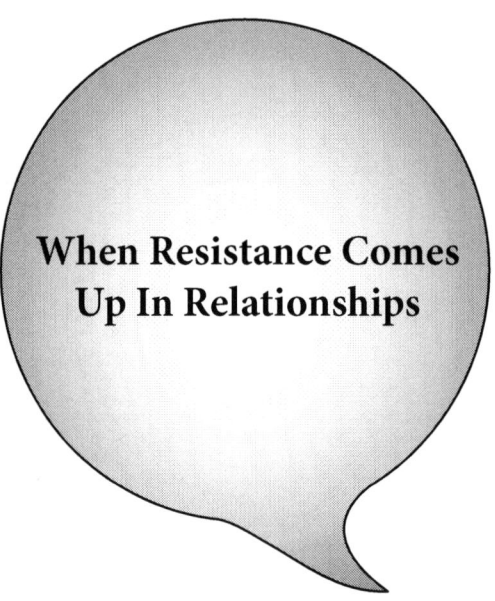

When Resistance Comes Up In Relationships

With everything you want to attract in a relationship, you are always going for *the vibrational match.*

It's a good idea to recognize when you have a vibrational match with a person in a relationship and when you do not.

Where you do not have a match, this is where you will start to *feel the resistance.* It becomes the distance between your vibration and someone eles's.

When you do not have a match you will feel out of alignment. You will notice you do not feel good.

1. My **INTENTION** for this week (around relationships, money, health, career and/or business) is …

_____
_____
_____
_____

2. Last week I felt **MOST GRATEFUL** for …

_____
_____
_____
_____

3. I **DELIBERATELY** used the Law of Attraction to attract…

_____
_____
_____
_____

4. I am **IN THE PROCESS** of manifesting…

_____
_____
_____
_____

5. I **FELT** major **POSITIVE VIBES** last week when …

_____
_____
_____
_____

THE
Ask ~ Believe ~ Receive
PROCESS

1. My **ASK** for this week is…

_____
_____
_____
_____

2. The **EVIDENCE** to support what I **BELIEVE** is possible looks like this…

_____
_____
_____
_____

3. I was excited to **RECEIVE** (fill in the blank) last week…

_____
_____
_____
_____

ABUNDANCE IS A FEELING

Make a list of all the ways you felt or observed
ABUNDANCE in your life last week…

_____	_____
_____	_____
_____	_____
_____	_____
_____	_____
_____	_____
_____	_____
_____	_____
_____	_____
_____	_____
_____	_____
_____	_____
_____	_____
_____	_____
_____	_____

WEEK 44

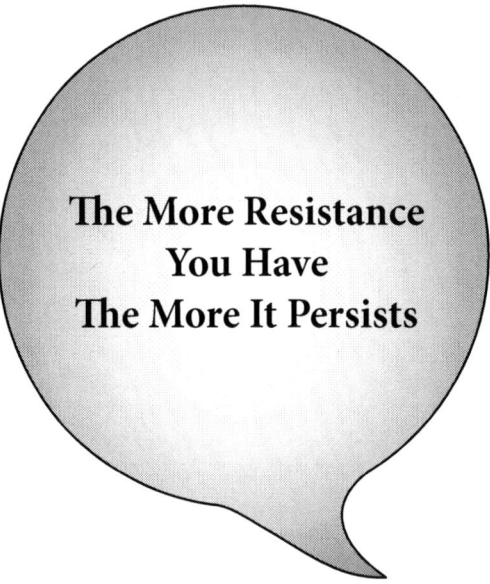

You've heard the expression 'what you think about, you bring about'. That's law of attraction 101, as is the expression *'the more you resist, the more it persists.'*

The reason for this is logical from the law of attraction perspective. Whatever you give your attention to, whether wanted or unwanted, you attract.

So it makes sense that if you continue to focus on the resistance, the more resistance you will attract. When you let go of the resistance, focus on something positive, you will attract that instead.

1. My **INTENTION** for this week (around relationships, money, health, career and/or business) is ...

_____
_____
_____
_____

2. Last week I felt **MOST GRATEFUL** for ...

_____
_____
_____
_____

3. I **DELIBERATELY** used the Law of Attraction to attract...

_____
_____
_____
_____

4. I am **IN THE PROCESS** of manifesting...

_____
_____
_____
_____

5. I **FELT** major **POSITIVE VIBES** last week when ...

_____
_____
_____
_____

THE
Ask ~ Believe ~ Receive
PROCESS

1. My **ASK** for this week is…

   _____
   _____
   _____
   _____

2. The **EVIDENCE** to support what I **BELIEVE** is possible looks like this…

   _____
   _____
   _____
   _____

3. I was excited to **RECEIVE** (fill in the blank) last week…

   _____
   _____
   _____
   _____

ABUNDANCE IS A FEELING

Make a list of all the ways you felt or observed
ABUNDANCE in your life last week…

_____   _____
_____   _____
_____   _____
_____   _____
_____   _____
_____   _____
_____   _____
_____   _____
_____   _____
_____   _____
_____   _____
_____   _____
_____   _____
_____   _____
_____   _____

Date: ____ / ____ / 20____

WEEK 45

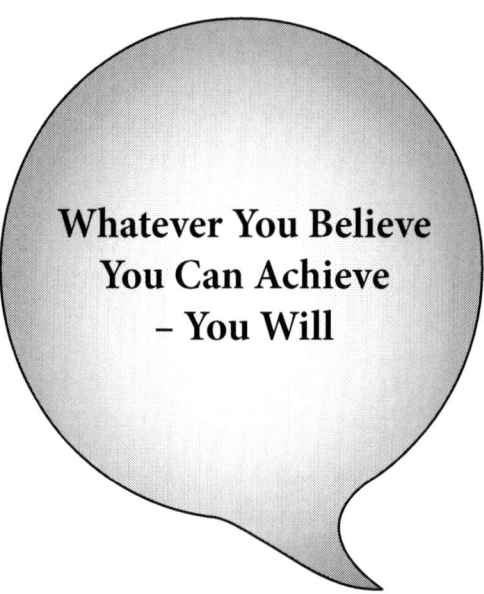

Whatever You Believe You Can Achieve – You Will

Everything in the world is energy. You are energy and the law of attraction is a strong energetic force that wants to work with you to bring you your desires for a happy, abundant life.

If you believe you can achieve something, you will

What you believe you can achieve requires that you have a positive mindset. Even if something seems to be standing in your way, go back to your intention. Stay positive. It's the law of attraction's job to send you vibrational matches to your desires.

1. My **INTENTION** for this week (around relationships, money, health, career and/or business) is …

2. Last week I felt **MOST GRATEFUL** for …

3. I **DELIBERATELY** used the Law of Attraction to attract…

4. I am **IN THE PROCESS** of manifesting…

5. I **FELT** major **POSITIVE VIBES** last week when …

THE
Ask ~ Believe ~ Receive
PROCESS

1. My **ASK** for this week is…

_____

_____

_____

_____

2. The **EVIDENCE** to support what I **BELIEVE** is possible looks like this…

_____

_____

_____

_____

3. I was excited to **RECEIVE** (fill in the blank) last week…

_____

_____

_____

_____

ABUNDANCE IS A FEELING

Make a list of all the ways you felt or observed
ABUNDANCE in your life last week…

Date: ____ /____ /20____

WEEK 46

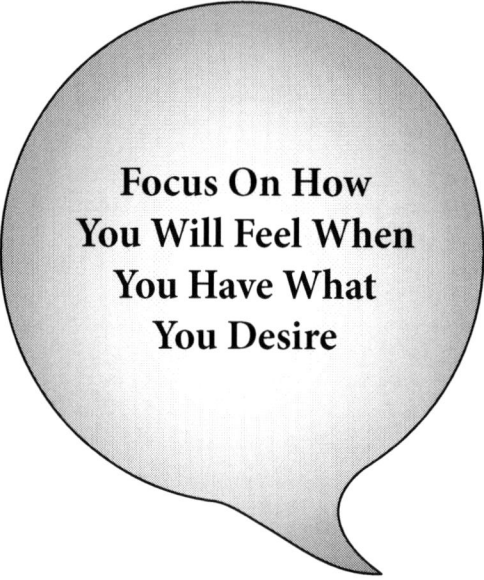

Focus On How You Will Feel When You Have What You Desire

One of the most important steps when you become a 'deliberate attractor' is to focus on *how you will feel* when your desires manifest.

You put your 'Ask' out into the Universe, you look for evidence to help you 'Believe' you can have what you want. Then you start to 'Receive' signs that you are attracting what you need to do, know or have. You continue to express gratitude.

Key to all of your manifesting is your positive or negative feelings about realizing your desires.

1. My **INTENTION** for this week (around relationships, money, health, career and/or business) is …

_____
_____
_____
_____

2. Last week I felt **MOST GRATEFUL** for …

_____
_____
_____
_____

3. I **DELIBERATELY** used the Law of Attraction to attract…

_____
_____
_____
_____

4. I am **IN THE PROCESS** of manifesting…

_____
_____
_____
_____

5. I **FELT** major **POSITIVE VIBES** last week when …

_____
_____
_____
_____

THE
Ask ~ Believe ~ Receive
PROCESS

1. My **ASK** for this week is…

   _____
   _____
   _____
   _____

2. The **EVIDENCE** to support what I **BELIEVE** is possible looks like this…

   _____
   _____
   _____
   _____

3. I was excited to **RECEIVE** (fill in the blank) last week…

   _____
   _____
   _____
   _____

ABUNDANCE IS A FEELING

Make a list of all the ways you felt or observed
ABUNDANCE in your life last week…

_____   _____
_____   _____
_____   _____
_____   _____
_____   _____
_____   _____
_____   _____
_____   _____
_____   _____
_____   _____
_____   _____
_____   _____
_____   _____
_____   _____
_____   _____

Date: ____ /____ /20____

WEEK 47

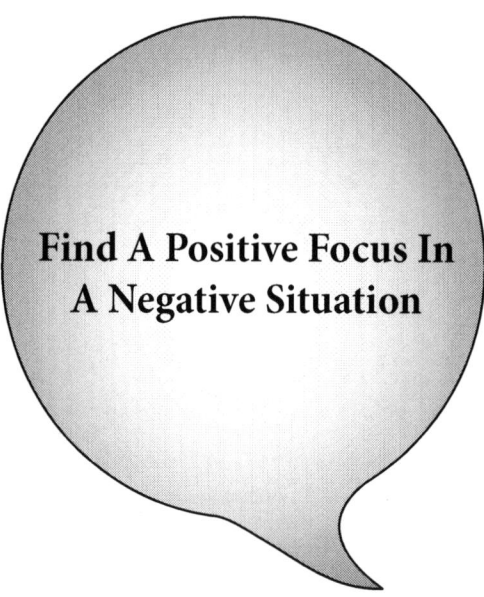

Find A Positive Focus In A Negative Situation

You may wonder how you can turn a negative situation into something positive because when you are in that situation you may not feel very positive.

As soon as you notice your negative thoughts, take a moment to find *just one positive thought about the person or the situation*. It might feel like a stretch for you but once you can get to one positive thought you will attract more positive thoughts.

You always want to be mindful of what you are putting in your vibrational bubble.

1. My **INTENTION** for this week (around relationships, money, health, career and/or business) is …

_____

_____

_____

_____

2. Last week I felt **MOST GRATEFUL** for …

_____

_____

_____

_____

3. I **DELIBERATELY** used the Law of Attraction to attract…

_____

_____

_____

_____

4. I am **IN THE PROCESS** of manifesting…

_____

_____

_____

_____

5. I **FELT** major **POSITIVE VIBES** last week when …

_____

_____

_____

_____

THE
Ask ~ Believe ~ Receive
PROCESS

1. My **ASK** for this week is…

_____
_____
_____
_____

2. The **EVIDENCE** to support what I **BELIEVE** is possible looks like this…

_____
_____
_____
_____

3. I was excited to **RECEIVE** (fill in the blank) last week…

_____
_____
_____
_____

ABUNDANCE IS A FEELING

Make a list of all the ways you felt or observed
ABUNDANCE in your life last week…

Date: ____ /____ /20____

WEEK 48

Let Go Of Beliefs That No Longer Serve You

Everyone has limiting beliefs that hold them back from feeling good. It takes a conscious effort to hear what you are saying to, or about yourself because it may be a habit for you.

Those limiting beliefs carry negative baggage that does not serve you. They don't make you happy and can be discouraging.

> A belief is a thought you think
> over and over

Find a replacement better-serving belief about yourself. Reframe the negative self-talk into something positive and put that in your vibrational bubble.

1. My **INTENTION** for this week (around relationships, money, health, career and/or business) is …

_____
_____
_____
_____

2. Last week I felt **MOST GRATEFUL** for …

_____
_____
_____
_____

3. I **DELIBERATELY** used the Law of Attraction to attract…

_____
_____
_____
_____

4. I am **IN THE PROCESS** of manifesting…

_____
_____
_____
_____

5. I **FELT** major **POSITIVE VIBES** last week when …

_____
_____
_____
_____

THE
Ask ~ Believe ~ Receive
PROCESS

1. My **ASK** for this week is…

2. The **EVIDENCE** to support what I **BELIEVE** is possible looks like this…

3. I was excited to **RECEIVE** (fill in the blank) last week…

ABUNDANCE IS A FEELING

Make a list of all the ways you felt or observed
ABUNDANCE in your life last week…

Date: ____ /____ /20____

WEEK 49

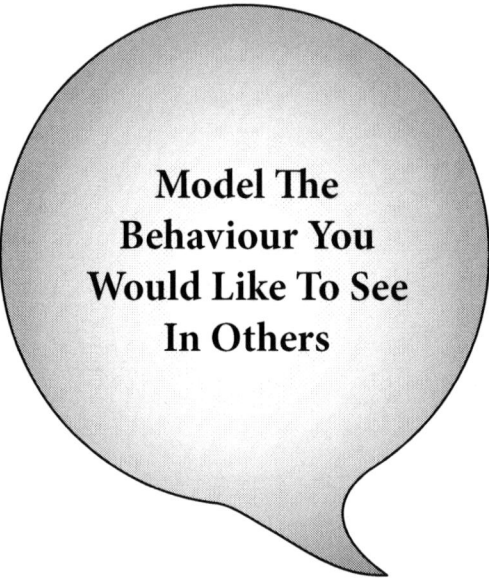

Model The Behaviour You Would Like To See In Others

You know that you can never change another person. You might even try to teach them about the law of attraction and share this Gratitude Journal with them to no avail.

Let the idea go that you can change someone and focus on being the best model for the behaviour you would like to see in others.

Show them

Telling them 'not to do this or not to do that' goes in one ear and out the other. Model the desired behaviour.

1. My **INTENTION** for this week (around relationships, money, health, career and/or business) is …

_____
_____
_____
_____

2. Last week I felt **MOST GRATEFUL** for …

_____
_____
_____
_____

3. I **DELIBERATELY** used the Law of Attraction to attract…

_____
_____
_____
_____

4. I am **IN THE PROCESS** of manifesting…

_____
_____
_____
_____

5. I **FELT** major **POSITIVE VIBES** last week when …

_____
_____
_____
_____

THE
Ask ~ Believe ~ Receive
PROCESS

1. My **ASK** for this week is…

_____
_____
_____
_____

2. The **EVIDENCE** to support what I **BELIEVE** is possible looks like this…

_____
_____
_____
_____

3. I was excited to **RECEIVE** (fill in the blank) last week…

_____
_____
_____
_____

ABUNDANCE IS A FEELING

Make a list of all the ways you felt or observed
ABUNDANCE in your life last week…

Date: ____ /____ /20____

WEEK 50

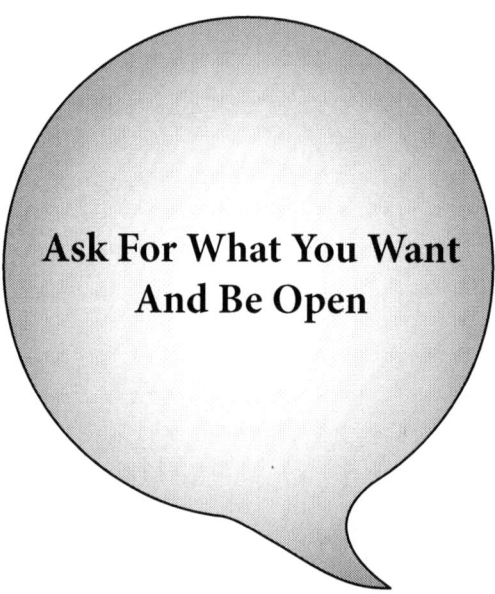

Ask For What You Want And Be Open

In the 'Ask Believe Receive' process you got crystal clear clarity on what it is you desire to manifest.

And, the law of attraction is going to give you what you need to do, know or have to help you manifest. Remove your doubt and allow the unfoldment.

But did you know that it responds really well when you put your 'Ask' out there and add…

*I'm open to this
or something better*

Try it and remember to express gratitude once you start the attracting process.

1. My **INTENTION** for this week (around relationships, money, health, career and/or business) is …

_____
_____
_____
_____

2. Last week I felt **MOST GRATEFUL** for …

_____
_____
_____
_____

3. I **DELIBERATELY** used the Law of Attraction to attract…

_____
_____
_____
_____

4. I am **IN THE PROCESS** of manifesting…

_____
_____
_____
_____

5. I **FELT** major **POSITIVE VIBES** last week when …

_____
_____
_____
_____

THE
Ask ~ Believe ~ Receive
PROCESS

1. My **ASK** for this week is…

_____
_____
_____
_____

2. The **EVIDENCE** to support what I **BELIEVE** is possible looks like this…

_____
_____
_____
_____

3. I was excited to **RECEIVE** (fill in the blank) last week…

_____
_____
_____
_____

ABUNDANCE IS A FEELING

Make a list of all the ways you felt or observed
ABUNDANCE in your life last week…

_____   _____
_____   _____
_____   _____
_____   _____
_____   _____
_____   _____
_____   _____
_____   _____
_____   _____
_____   _____
_____   _____
_____   _____
_____   _____

Date: ____ /____ /20____

WEEK 51

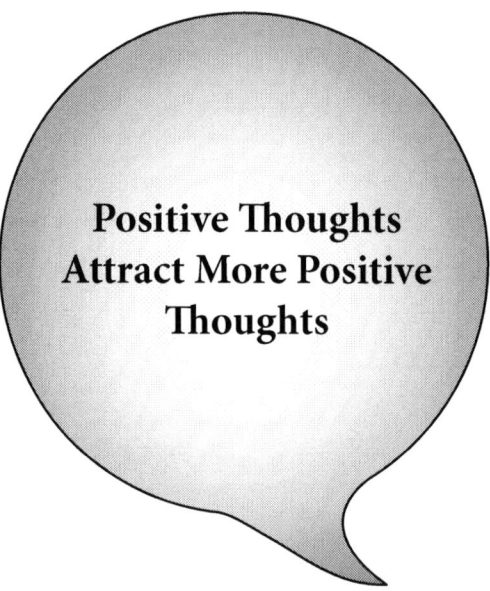

Positive Thoughts Attract More Positive Thoughts

When you give your attention, energy or focus to something whether wanted or unwanted you attract more of the same.

Typically the thoughts you are having around what you *do want to attract* carry a positive vibe. And now that you understand the job description of the law of attraction – to match vibrations – you now understand how to deliberately attract more positive people, things or situations that also come with positive vibes.

Keep your thoughts positive and if you slip, just remember to reset your vibe.

1. My **INTENTION** for this week (around relationships, money, health, career and/or business) is …

   _____
   _____
   _____
   _____

2. Last week I felt **MOST GRATEFUL** for …

   _____
   _____
   _____
   _____

3. I **DELIBERATELY** used the Law of Attraction to attract…

   _____
   _____
   _____
   _____

4. I am **IN THE PROCESS** of manifesting…

   _____
   _____
   _____
   _____

5. I **FELT** major **POSITIVE VIBES** last week when …

   _____
   _____
   _____
   _____

THE
Ask ~ Believe ~ Receive
PROCESS

1. My **ASK** for this week is…

_____
_____
_____
_____

2. The **EVIDENCE** to support what I **BELIEVE** is possible looks like this…

_____
_____
_____
_____

3. I was excited to **RECEIVE** (fill in the blank) last week…

_____
_____
_____
_____

ABUNDANCE IS A FEELING

Make a list of all the ways you felt or observed
ABUNDANCE in your life last week…

_____	_____
_____	_____
_____	_____
_____	_____
_____	_____
_____	_____
_____	_____
_____	_____
_____	_____
_____	_____
_____	_____
_____	_____
_____	_____
_____	_____
_____	_____

Date: ____ / ____ / 20____

WEEK 52

Celebrate Your Success

You get to decide what 'success' looks like to you and it only matters what *you think*.

One of the best ways to raise your vibration is to focus on your success. Big, small, doesn't matter ...

Celebrate your success

Do whatever makes you feel good. It might be your happy dance, glass of wine, high-five someone or yourself, buy something special that reminds you of your success.

Keep happy thoughts in your vibrational bubble to pull out when you want to feel good!

1. My **INTENTION** for this week (around relationships, money, health, career and/or business) is …

_____
_____
_____
_____

2. Last week I felt **MOST GRATEFUL** for …

_____
_____
_____
_____

3. I **DELIBERATELY** used the Law of Attraction to attract…

_____
_____
_____
_____

4. I am **IN THE PROCESS** of manifesting…

_____
_____
_____
_____

5. I **FELT** major **POSITIVE VIBES** last week when …

_____
_____
_____
_____

THE
Ask ~ Believe ~ Receive
PROCESS

1. My **ASK** for this week is…

   _____
   _____
   _____
   _____

2. The **EVIDENCE** to support what I **BELIEVE** is possible looks like this…

   _____
   _____
   _____
   _____

3. I was excited to **RECEIVE** (fill in the blank) last week…

   _____
   _____
   _____
   _____

ABUNDANCE IS A FEELING

Make a list of all the ways you felt or observed
ABUNDANCE in your life last week…

WHAT I DISCOVERED ABOUT MYSELF, GRATITUDE *and* THE LAW OF ATTRACTION

ABOUT THE AUTHOR

Dana Smithers

Author, speaker, international Certified Law of Attraction trainer

Dana J. Smithers known as the 'How To Law of Attraction Gal' has been using the Law of Attraction since she was 35 years old when she started on her spiritual journey to turn her unhappy life around. She remembers the time when she was broke, divorced, working in another country and with a man she no longer respected. Once she had her 'ah ha' moment and started 'deliberately' using the Law of Attraction in her life her relationships, her money story, her health and her career transformed from negatives into positives.

At the age of 50 she left a successful and well paying human resources corporate job of 20+ years to pursue her dream of creating beautiful spaces for people. Interestingly enough she never wanted to be an 'entrepreneur'. While she thought at the time that she just 'fell into it' she later learned from the law of attraction perspective that she attracted it! Fast forward her interior decorating career, home staging became popular so she started offering home staging services and then started her own professional home staging training course. She eventually sold that by using the '3 Step Deliberate Attraction' process and then focused her attention on becoming a coach and mentor to women solopreneurs. Also at the age of 50 she decided she wanted to find a life partner after being divorced for 20 years, she used the' 3 Step Deliberate Attraction' process and within 5 months met her husband-to-be!

She believes the journey to living a happy and fulfilled life is found through your mind-body-spirit connection. As a Certified Law of Attraction Trainer she teaches her clients how to use LOA tools and processes to create what they desire by working on their 'mind'. As a Certified Sacred Gifts Guide she helps women discover their sacred gifts so they feel more connected to 'spirit' and are aligned and 'feel on purpose'. Being an Emotion Code Practitioner allows Dana to release negative trapped emotions lodged in the 'body' that are holding people back from living a happier, more fulfilled life.

She invites you to sign up for her FREE enewsletter for tips, insights and inspiration and her FREE ebook *'The POWER of your WORDS'* at www.DanaSmithers.com. She looks forward to making a real connection with you on **www.FB.com/coachdanasmithers.**

Dana Smithers lives in Vancouver, Canada

www.DanaSmithers.com

Made in the USA
Columbia, SC
18 April 2017